The Hebrew Bible

The Hebrew Bible

Feminist and Intersectional Perspectives

GALE A. YEE, EDITOR

FORTRESS PRESS
MINNEAPOLIS

THE HEBREW BIBLE
Feminist and Intersectional Perspectives

Cover image: Ruth and Naomi / He Qi
Cover design: Laurie Ingram

Print ISBN: 978-1-5064-2548-1
eBook ISBN: 978-1-5064-2549-8

The paper used in this publication meets the minimum requirements of American National Standard for Information Sciences — Permanence of Paper for Printed Library Materials, ANSI Z329.48-1984.

Manufactured in the U.S.A.

Contents

Part III. Prophecy

Part IV. The Writings

Preface

This book is intended to be a supplement to standard introductions to the Hebrew Bible/Old Testament, highlighting key issues of interpretation from feminist and intersectional perspectives that have arisen particularly during the last fifty-five years. They include sociohistorical, literary, and interdisciplinary analyses of the Bible, viewed through the interconnected lenses of gender, race/ethnicity, class, the so-called third world, and colonial status, which are often absent from these introductions.

This book is intended for advanced undergraduate and graduate students in seminaries and universities, as well as interested lay readers. Six female biblical scholars, who have years of experience teaching introductory courses to the Bible under their belt, contribute to this volume. As the editor of the volume, I will begin by familiarizing the reader with feminist, intersectional scholarship in general, and then will highlight some of the feminist and intersectional analyses of important feminist biblical scholars and the interpretive methods they use. In part 1, Carolyn J. Sharp will undertake the study of the first five books of the Bible, the Torah/ Pentateuch. Vanessa Lovelace will devote her chapter to the Deuteronomistic History (Joshua—Kings) in part 2. Part 3, Prophecy, will be in the able hands of Corrine Carvalho. Finally, two scholars, Melody D. Knowles and Judy Fentress-Williams, will share the investigation of the Writings in part 4.

Each of the four chapters dealing with the Hebrew Bible contains an overview that addresses feminist and intersectional contributions raised in its specific division. The chapters are meant to be introductory and not exhaustive, raising the students' consciousness of the issues and directing them to where they can learn more. The following are some of the questions and comments that have actually been raised by our students:

- Why is God always male?

- What does it mean when God said, "Let US make THEM in OUR own image"?

- Why are there historical tales of queens and empresses often from other cultures, while the main characters in the Hebrew Bible are predominantly men?

- What is the woman's version of the Hebrew Bible? Would women have told these stories from the same slant?

- What happened to Bathsheba sounds like stalking, peeping-tom stuff, coupled with sexual assault and murder. Is it?

- We read all kinds of violence in the Hebrew Bible, and the violence against women is especially distressing. Why don't we hear about these stories in our churches?

- Esther is in a threatening situation with Ahasuerus, and according to the book of Esther, that's all part of God's larger plan. So, are we saying that God purposefully puts women at risk of sexual violation or death? That's theologically very problematic.

- So often women of color are portrayed as evil or immoral in white culture. How can we know that Jezebel actually was evil? What if the Bible's picture of Jezebel was just as distorted as some of the news coverage we see about black people today?

- Why do the prophets always blame women for what happens?

- When feminists critique the androcentrism in the Latter Prophets, does that make feminists into "false prophets"? It's not fair that, in order to resist what is harmful in the prophets, we have to stand against God's word. The dilemma is maddening.

- What do I do with this information? Now that I know how misogynistic biblical authors could be, and now that I am repulsed by some of the things I read, how did this book ever become Sacred Scripture? Why should I read it now? Who could "believe" in this stuff?

This volume will not answer all of your students' feminist and intersectional questions. More important in the learning process are the students' questions themselves and their lively "wrestling" with the difficult issues that they encounter in their reading.[1] The Bible has been a foundational text for prescribing various beliefs on many social relations of power: male/female, master/slave, rich/poor, colonizer/colonized, native/immigrant, white/nonwhite, heterosexual/homosexual, believer/unbeliever, and so forth. Its views were often oppressive for subordinate populations, negating the *shalom* that the Scriptures themselves promised. We hope that this volume will help your students learn how feminist and intersectional biblical scholarship has engaged these questions to assist them in their own "wrestling" with these issues.

---

1. Carolyn J. Sharp, *Wrestling the Word: The Hebrew Scriptures and the Christian Believer* (Louisville: Westminster John Knox, 2010).

Introduction: Definitions, Explorations, and Intersections

GALE A. YEE

DEFINITIONS

The Bible has been a foundational text, not only for the religious communities of Jews and Christians, but particularly for its influence in the formation and perpetuation of certain gender relations that privileged men and disenfranchised women. Serious critique against this inequality between the genders arose particularly in the latter half of the twentieth century by the proponents of feminism and intersectionality and continues in the present day. Let's begin this introductory essay by defining "feminism" and "intersectionality," the major themes of this book. After this, I will present a short history of the women's movement and the various modes of feminist theorizing, and then turn to feminist and intersectional perspectives on the Bible.

In its most general sense, the word "feminism" refers to the political activism by women on behalf of women.[1] When used in biblical studies, feminist criticism is one of a series of recent methods of biblical exegesis (interpretation) that fall under the term "ideological criticism." The ideological criticisms investigate the power differentials in certain social relationships in the production of the text (who wrote it, when, and why), how these power relations are reproduced in the text itself, and how they are consumed by

1. Carole R. McCann and Seung-Kyung Kim, eds., "Introduction: Feminist Theory, Local and Global Perspectives," in *Feminist Theory Reader: Local and Global Perspectives*, 4th ed. (New York: Routledge, 2017), 1.

readers of various social groups. For example, materialist criticism (aka Marxist or socioeconomic criticism) investigates ideologies of economic class relations that keep certain classes wealthier and others poorer. Postcolonial criticism looks at relations between colonizer and colonized and the ideologies that keep the conquerors and the natives in their respective places. Cultural criticism examines the ideologies of how the Bible was received and used in high and popular culture throughout the ages and globally. And so, for our purposes, feminist criticism studies the ideologies of gender that legitimize unequal relations between men and women. Many schools of thought exist in feminist studies, such as liberal feminism, radical feminism, Marxist/socialist feminism, postmodern feminism, psychoanalytic feminism, postcolonial feminism, feminisms of color, ecofeminism, to name a few.[2] This rich diversity of feminist thinking will be reflected in the various theoretical approaches of feminist biblical scholars.

"Intersectionality" was a term coined in 1989 by the African American lawyer Kimberlé Crenshaw to theorize the complex interconnections between gender, race, and class that have marginalized black and nonwhite women in the subjugation they routinely experienced. Rich white men experience "oppression" differently from poor women of color, because both occupy different but intersected and often conflicted locations on gender, race, and class continuums. These interconnections, however, had been explored by African American theorists long before the term became fashionable.[3] Moreover, intersectional interfaces have sometimes been broadened theoretically to include other categories of analysis along with gender, race, and class, such as sexuality, colonial status, ethnicity, physical ability, and so forth.[4]

---

2. Rosemarie Tong, *Feminist Thought: A More Comprehensive Introduction*, 4th ed. (Boulder, CO: Westview, 2014).

3. Cf. the Combahee River Collective, "A Black Feminist Statement," in *Capitalist Patriarchy and the Case for Social Feminism*, ed. Zillah Eisenstein (New York: Monthly Review, 1978), 362–72; Angela Y. Davis, *Women, Race and Class* (New York: Vintage, 1981); bell hooks, *Feminist Theory: From Margin to Center* (Boston: South End, 1984).

4. Sumi Cho, Kimberlé Williams Crenshaw, and Leslie McCall, "Toward a Field of Intersectionality Studies: Theory, Applications, and Praxis," *Signs: Journal of Women in Culture & Society* 38, no. 4 (Summer 2013): 785–810; Bonnie Thornton Dill and Ruth Enid Zambrana, "Critical Thinking about Inequality: An Emerging Lens," in *Feminist Theory Reader: Local and Global Perspectives*, ed. Carol R McCann and Seung-Kyung Kim, 4th ed. (New York: Routledge, 2017), 182–93. First published 2009.

CAN WOMEN BECOME LIKE MEN? DO WOMEN WANT TO? SHOULD THEY WANT TO?

The feminist movement has often been described through the metaphor of "waves."[5] The first wave possibly began in the eighteenth century with the treatise by Mary Wollstonecraft, *A Vindication of the Rights of Women*, who argued that the dependence of (privileged) women on men kept them in their homes and deprived them of becoming educated and being independent rational agents like men. The movement toward women's rights continued in the nineteenth century with the women's suffrage movement through other liberal feminists, such as Sarah and Angelina Grimké, Lucretia Mott, and Elizabeth Cady Stanton. The so-called second wave of US feminism began during the politically turbulent 1960s, sparked by the publication of Betty Friedan's *The Feminist Mystique* and the formation of the National Organization for Women (NOW) and other liberal feminist women's rights groups. Liberal feminism advocated equal rights for women in employment, education, reproduction, and other legal matters. Some of its gains were the right to vote, to education, to work outside the home, access to birth control and legalized abortion, the enactment of affirmative action laws, and laws against sexual and domestic violence. However, liberal feminism primarily advanced the concerns of white, heterosexual, middle-class, educated women and neglected the concerns of poor women of color. Furthermore, it made being "male" the ideal by presuming that women could become like men if they wanted to, that women wanted to become like men, and that they should want to become like men.[6]

However, for many women, becoming male was not the ideal to be strived for. Rather, the sexism and misogyny of men was the very source of their oppression. The radical feminists criticized the "rights" focus in the liberal feminist agenda, because they did not think that women's oppression would be eliminated simply by changing the laws, educating women, and letting them have careers

---

5. However, the "waves" metaphor has been criticized particularly because it tended to exclude white anti-racist women and women of color in the typical histories of the women's movement. See Linda Nicholson, "Feminism in 'Waves': Useful Metaphor or Not?," in *Feminist Theory Reader: Local and Global Perspectives*, ed. Carol R. McCann and Seung-Kyung Kim, 4th ed. (New York: Routledge, 2017), 182–93. First published 2010.

6. See chapter 1 on "Liberal Feminism" in Tong, *Feminist Thought*, 11–49.

outside the home. Women's oppression went much deeper because it was embedded in a male system characterized by power, dominance, hierarchy, and competition. According to Andrea Dworkin, "Sexism is the foundation on which all tyranny is built. Every social form of hierarchy and abuse is modeled on male-over-female domination." Investigating the biblical text as embedded in a patriarchal system that subordinated women would be influential in the work of feminist biblical scholars, as we will see.

A good starting point to understand the different forms of radical feminism is the essay by Gayle Rubin, "The Traffic in Women." Rubin traced the roots of women's oppression by analyzing the male thinkers Karl Marx, Claude Lévi-Strauss, Sigmund Freud, and Jacques Lacan on how they theorized what she called "the sex/gender system." The sex/gender system "is the set of arrangements by which a society transforms biological sexuality into products of human activity."[7] Sex referred to one's biological anatomy; gender referred to the social constructions based on one's biological anatomy. Patriarchy[8] took certain aspects related to male and female physical biology (such as, men are stronger than women, women have no penis) to construct gendered identities of maleness and femaleness and social arrangements that served to empower men and disempower women. Patriarchy convinced men and women that these social constructions of gender were somehow "natural," "essential," or "normal," and any deviance from them was "evil" and "abnormal." Using these constructions to give themselves power and authority, men kept women under their control. Women became objects of exchange by men "given in marriage, taken in battle, exchanged for favors, sent as tribute, traded, bought and sold."[9]

This conceptual separation of sex from gender helps us understand the different forms of radical feminism and their contrasting views on how to combat sexism. Radical-libertarian feminists believed that just focusing on female gender identity would limit their development as full human persons. They encouraged women to become androgynous, encouraging both masculine and feminine characteristics. This view worked on the presumption that male

---

7. Gayle Rubin, "The Traffic in Women: Notes on the 'Political Economy' of Sex," in *Toward an Anthropology of Women*, ed. Rayna R. Reiter (New York: Monthly Review, 1975), 159.

8. Patriarchy refers to a social system where males dominate and have authority over women as a group. It has a literal sense of "rule of the father" in kinship societies such as ancient Israel's, where power in the family resides in the oldest living male, usually the father.

9. Rubin, "The Traffic in Women," 175.

characteristics were aggressive, independent, and competitive, while female characteristics were compassionate, nurturing, and obedient. The radical-cultural feminist theologian Mary Daly scoffed at the notion of androgyny for women, as "John Travolta and Farrah Fawcett-Majors scotch-taped together" (or George Clooney and Beyoncé taped together). Radical-cultural feminists saw men and women as *essentially different* and wanted to reassert values of female culture that have been suppressed by male culture. Some radical-cultural feminists would go so far as advocating the overthrow of the existing male order and creating a new society governed by the supposedly superior ethics of the female. Unlike liberal feminists who advocated sexual equality, these feminists believed that women were superior to men.[10]

From this point on, I will be discussing the ensuing forms of feminism rather quickly, touching mainly on feminist thought that has influenced feminist biblical scholars. Marxist feminists identified two systems oppressing women, class exploitation and patriarchy, examining the ways in which they colluded in subjugating women and where their interests collided.[11] They sharpened Marx's understanding of ideology[12] in the cultural production of gender in sophisticated ways.[13] They were particularly important in developing standpoint theory, which presumed that all knowledge was constructed from situated positions within different social locations that influenced how people viewed the world, such as different race, gender, and class positions. Like the standpoint of the proletariat in Marxist theory, Hartsock argued that women's lives offered a particular vantage point that could provide a powerful critique of patriarchal institutions.[14] Standpoint theory and epistemology (how

10. For fuller discussions of the streams of radical-feminist thought, see Tong, *Feminist Thought*, 50–92; Susan Archer Mann, *Doing Feminist Theory: From Modernity to Postmodernity* (Oxford: Oxford University Press, 2012), 78–111.

11. Heidi Hartmann, "The Unhappy Marriage of Marxism and Feminism: Towards a More Progressive Union," in *The Second Wave: A Reader in Feminist Theory*, ed. Linda Nicholson (New York: Routledge, 1997), 97–122. First published 1981.

12. Ideology is a complex system of meaning that constructs "reality" for people and helps them understand their place in the world as natural, inevitable, and necessary. It is not "reality" itself.

13. Michèle Barrett, *Women's Oppression Today: The Marxist/Feminist Encounter*, rev. ed. (London: Verso, 1988).

14. Nancy C. M. Hartsock, "The Feminist Standpoint: Toward a Specifically Feminist Historical Materialism," in *Feminist Theory Reader: Local and Global Perspectives*, ed. Carol R. McCann and Seung-Kyung Kim, 4th ed. (New York: Routledge, 2017), 368–83. First published 1983.

we know what we know) contested the prevailing views of scientific knowledge as objective, value-free, or neutral. They would become especially important when feminists of color developed their own theories of situational knowledge and of women's oppression.

Another reaction to the views of knowledge as objective and value-free were the postmodern feminisms.[15] In postmodern theory, social reality and human subjectivity (one's sense of self) were formed in and through language. What we know about the world and ourselves was defined and contested in the language of historically specific discourses. Discourse broadly referred to the various symbolic and linguistic systems and narratives used in human communication, such as legal discourse, political discourse, medical discourse, and right-wing discourse. There was no "reality" or "real world" because what we thought was "real" was known only through different and often conflicting discourses. What became socially or culturally legitimated as knowledge resulted from specific maneuvers by those in power who controlled the discourse, such as the institutional church regarding matters of belief. A shift thus occurs in theory from "*What* truth is being claimed and what truth is being suppressed?" to "*Whose* truth is being claimed and whose truth is being suppressed?" "Truth" was not objective; rather "truth" was what the dominant discourse maintained it to be. However, other suppressed voices, such as women's, had this tendency to make "truth" unstable and slippery. Postmodern feminists claimed that there was not a single discourse of gender or sexuality but multiple and competing discourses. The gender identity of one's maleness and femaleness became the site of continual conflicts among discourses, such as religious discourse, medical discourse, literary discourse, right-wing discourse, liberal or radical feminist discourse, and so on, for the allegiance of its subjects. Gender or maleness and femaleness did not exist outside of discourses. Determining what gender *was* depended on which discourse was attempting to define it and then analyzing the dominant powers that controlled it.[16]

Emerging in the 1990s, queer theory was an amalgam of

15. Postmodernism has been used interchangeably with poststructuralism, although poststructuralism applies narrowly to five French theorists: Jacques Derrida, Michel Foucault, Jacques Lacan, Julia Kristeva, and Roland Barthes.

16. For fuller discussions of postmodern feminisms see Carol R. McCann and Seung-Kyung Kim, eds., "Introduction: Theorizing Feminist Knowledge and Agency," in *Feminist Theory Reader: Local and Global Perspectives*, 4th ed. (New York: Routledge, 2017), 358–65; Tong, *Feminist Thought*, 192–210.

postmodernism, feminist theory, and gay/lesbian studies. Postmodernism argued that all language was composed of binary pairs of opposition, like white/black, heaven/hell, soul/body, male/female, saved/sinner. The problem with binaries was that one part of the binary was privileged over the other. Queer theorists wanted to subvert the binaries of male/female and heterosexual/homosexual by highlighting gender and sexual fluidity. Taking her cues from Simone de Beauvoir's assertion that "one is not born, but, rather *becomes* a woman," Judith Butler argued that because of its instability, gender was "an identity instituted through a *stylized repetition of acts.*"[17] Gender came into being through the repeated performances of acts, norms, and conventions associated with heterosexual maleness and femaleness, such as wearing pants for men and dresses for women. Typifying postmodern thinking and applying it to a transvestite on stage, Butler asserted:

> If the "reality" of gender is constituted by the performance itself, then there is no recourse to an essential and unrealized "sex" or "gender" which gender performances ostensibly express. Indeed, the transvestite's gender is as fully real as anyone whose performance complies with social expectations. Gender reality is performative which means, quite simply, that it is real only to the extent that it is performed.[18]

Sexualities themselves were socially constructed in queer feminist thinking.[19] According to Gayle Rubin, whom we encountered before, many sexualities and sexual expressions did not fit into the strict male/female and heterosexual/homosexual binaries and were regulated by societies and cultures in hierarchies of sexual value.[20] This observation became the basis for queer analyses of heteronormativity: the assumption that heterosexuality is "natural," "normal," and "right," privileging and institutionalizing heterosexuality as the "correct" form of sexual relations, and defining

17. Judith Butler, "Performative Acts and Gender Constitution: An Essay in Phenomenology and Feminist Theory," in *Feminist Theory Reader: Local and Global Perspectives*, ed. Carol R. McCann and Seung-Kyung Kim, 4th ed. (New York: Routledge, 2017), 481. First published 1988.
18. Butler, "Performative Acts and Gender Constitution," 488–89.
19. Mann, *Doing Feminist Theory*, 235–38.
20. Gayle Rubin, "Thinking Sex: Notes for a Radical Theory of the Politics of Sexuality," in *Pleasure and Danger: Exploring Female Sexuality* (Boston: Routledge & Kegan Paul, 1984), 267–319. The following is a list of Rubin's non-normative sexualities: homosexual, unmarried, promiscuous, nonprocreative, commercial, alone or in groups, casual, cross-generational, in public, pornographic, with manufactured objects, sadomasochistic (281).

other sexual forms as "bad" and "unnatural." "Like gender, sexuality is political. It is organized into systems of power, which reward and encourage some individuals and activities, while punishing and suppressing others."[21]

THEORIZING INTERSECTING IDENTITIES

We believe that sexual politics under patriarchy is as pervasive in black women's lives as are the politics of class and race. We also often find it difficult to separate race from class from sex oppression because in our lives they are most often experienced simultaneously. We know that there is such a thing as racial-sexual oppression, which is neither solely racial nor solely sexual. . . . We need to articulate the real class situation of persons who are not merely raceless, sexless workers, but for whom racial and sexual oppression are significant determinants in their working/economic lives.[22]

African American feminists, such as the Combahee River Collective just cited, have long noted the interconnections among gender, race, class, and sexuality in the early days of the women's movement. They observed that they were oppressed as blacks in a society dominated by whites, as women in a patriarchal society and by the civil rights and black power movements, which were run mostly by men, and as lesbians in a society where heteronormativity was standard.

It took a while, however, for white feminists to catch on to such intersections. In an important study, Elizabeth Spelman critiqued the essentialist arguments of some important white feminists, who claimed that sexism was a more fundamental form of oppression than racism.[23] Citing Lorraine Bethel's colorful exclamation, "What Chou Mean WE, White Girl?"[24] Spelman remarked that it was not surprising that women of color have been distrustful of white women, who pointed out their commonalities when it seemed politically expedient to do, but overlooked their dissimilarities. In trying to argue that all women shared the same oppression under patriarchy, white feminists neglected to consider the differences among women in their presumption of "sameness." They seemed

21. Rubin, "Thinking Sex," 309.

22. The Combahee River Collective, "A Black Feminist Statement," 117. First published 1978.

23. Elizabeth V. Spelman, *Inessential Woman: Problems of Exclusion in Feminist Thought* (Boston: Beacon, 1988), 114–32.

24. Lorraine Bethel, "What Chou Mean WE, White Girl?" *Conditions* 5 (1979): 86–92.

to assume that *all* women shared their white, middle-class, educated social locations.[25] White feminists often invoked the notion of "sisterhood" to mobilize women politically and stress women's common concerns. However, according to Audre Lorde, "There is a pretense to homogeneity of experience covered by the word *sisterhood* that does not in fact exist. . . . Certainly there are very real differences between us of race, age, and sex. But it is not those differences between us that are separating us. It is rather our refusal to recognize those differences."[26] She described her social location as a black, female, lesbian mother of a daughter and a son, poet, and partner in a racially mixed relationship as a "sister outsider."

Before recognizing intersectionality as a critical aspect of feminist theory, white feminists had different ways of dealing with multiple oppressions. As Spelman pointed out, one model was to rank oppressions in a hierarchy, treating one form of oppression as earlier or more fundamental than others. Recall Andrea Dworkin's claim above that "sexism is the foundation on which all tyranny is built. Every social form of hierarchy and abuse is modeled on male-over-female domination." Some Marxist feminists privileged class oppression, with gender and race oppressions as less important derivatives. Another way of dealing with multiple oppressions was known variously as the "tootsie roll," "pop-bead," and "ampersand" approach.[27] This was an additive model in which multiple oppressions, such as racism, sexism, and classism, were treated as separate and distinct. Oppressions were simply added together and people just described as doubly or triply subjugated.

Neither model adequately dealt with the reality that oppressions formed an integrated whole with each continually interwoven with the other. The Combahee River Collective, cited above, described the interconnectedness of oppressions as occurring "simultaneously." Kimberlé Crenshaw described it as "intersectionality," which highlighted the fact that women of color were situated within at least two subordinated groups that frequently pursued conflicting political agendas. She noted that the experiences of black women were assumed to be synonymous with either black males by anti-

25. Spelman, *Inessential Woman*, 138–39, fn 6.

26. Audre Lorde, *Sister Outsider: Essays and Speeches by Audre Lorde* (Freedom, CA: The Crossing Press, 1984), 115–16.

27. Spelman, *Inessential Woman*, 114–15, 136–37; Deborah King, "Multiple Jeopardy: The Context of a Black Feminist Ideology," in *Feminist Frameworks*, ed. Alison M. Jaggar and Paula S. Rothenberg, 3rd ed. (Boston: McGraw-Hill, 1993), 220–36. First published 1988.

racist strategies or with white women by feminist ones. The single-issue focus of these strategies ignored the full dimension of racist and sexist oppression experienced by women of color.[28]

African American feminist Patricia Hill Collins developed Crenshaw's intersectionality with her own theory of the "matrix of domination."

> Intersectional paradigms remind us that oppression cannot be reduced to one fundamental type, and that oppressions work together in producing injustice. In contrast, the matrix of domination refers to how these intersecting oppressions are actually organized.[29]

According to Collins, any particular matrix of domination was organized through four interrelated domains of power: the *structural* (institutional structures of society), the *disciplinary* (ideas and practices that characterized and sustained bureaucratic hierarchies), the *hegemonic* (the ideas, symbols, and ideologies that shaped consciousness), and the *interpersonal* (the interactions of people at the macro- and micro-levels of social organization).[30] "Each domain serves a particular purpose. The structural domain organizes oppression, whereas the disciplinary domain manages it. The hegemonic domain justifies oppression, and the interpersonal domain influences everyday lived experience and the individual conscious-ness that ensues."[31] In the politics of power and empowerment, people could simultaneously be both oppressors and oppressed, powerful and powerless, because of their different and shifting locations in a matrix of domination. For example, June Jordan meditated on being an African American female in the Sheraton British Colonial Hotel in the Bahamas, being serviced by lower-class Afro-Caribbean maids, waiters, and market vendors. Even though in the United States, she would endure systemic racism for her blackness, she was privileged in race and class compared to the service workers in the Bahamas.[32] Collins argued that black feminism needed to develop more complex notions of empowerment and resistance,

28. Kimberlé Williams Crenshaw, "Mapping the Margins: Intersectionality, Identity Politics, and Violence Against Women of Color," in *Critical Race Theory: The Key Writings That Formed the Movement*, ed. Kimberlé Crenshaw et al. (New York: New Press, 1995), 357–83.

29. Patricia Hill Collins, *Black Feminist Thought: Knowledge, Consciousness, and the Politics of Empowerment*, 2nd ed. (New York: Routledge, 2009), 21.

30. Collins, *Black Feminist Thought*, 295–307.

31. Collins, *Black Feminist Thought*, 294.

32. June Jordan, "Report from the Bahamas," in *Feminist Theory Reader: Local and Global*

by being cognizant of the ways in which a matrix of domination was structured through those interrelated domains of power. The simplistic model of oppressors and oppressed did not adequately deal with the complexity of the matrix of domination, which worked not only along certain axes—race, gender, class, sexuality—but also through the four interconnected domains of power.[33]

African American feminists were not alone in theorizing the intersections of gender, race, class, and sexualities. Asian American[34] and Latina American feminists have also been actively involved since the 1960s and 70s on behalf of their constituencies.[35] This short history can only name a few of their number. Lisa Lowe's highly anthologized "Heterogeneity, Hybridity, Multiplicity: Asian American Differences" was a landmark essay highlighting the fact that although Asian Americans differed from white Anglo society, they were extremely different and diverse from the perspectives of Asian Americans themselves. Heterogeneity, hybridity, and multiplicity signified the material contradictions that characterized Asian American groups that disrupted the dominant discursive construction of Asian Americans as a homogeneous group.[36] Gloria Anzaldúa and Cherríe Moraga were two Chicana (Mexican American) feminists, who brought to the forefront of feminist theory the writings of third-world women in their trailblazing anthology, *This Bridge Called My Back: Writings by Radical Women of Color*.[37] In *Borderlands/La Frontera*, Anzaldúa used English and Spanish to highlight the linguistic dislocations that characterized the Latina American feminist experience. She also developed the notion of "borderlands," such as the US/Mexican border, as an important epistemological location to critique US colonialism, heteronormativity, and male dominance.[38]

Perspectives, ed. Carol R. McCann and Seung-Kyung Kim, 4th ed. (New York: Routledge, 2017), 304–12. First published 1985.

33. Collins, *Black Feminist Thought*, 308.

34. See Leslie Bow, ed., *Asian American Feminisms* (London: Routledge, 2013) for the most up-to-date anthology of Asian American feminisms.

35. Becky Thompson, "Multiracial Feminism: Recasting the Chronology of Second Wave Feminism," in *Feminist Theory Reader: Local and Global Perspectives*, ed. Carol R. McCann and Seung-Kyung Kim, 4th ed. (New York: Routledge, 2017), 51–62. First published 2002.

36. Lisa Lowe, "Heterogeneity, Hybridity, Multiplicity: Marking Asian American Difference," *Diaspora* 1 (1991): 24–44.

37. Cherríe Moraga and Gloria Anzaldúa, eds., *This Bridge Called My Back: Writings by Radical Women of Color* (New York: Kitchen Table: Women of Color Press, 1981).

38. Gloria Anzaldúa, *Borderlands: La Frontera: The New Mestiza*, 4th ed. (San Francisco: Aunt Lute Books, 2012). First published 1999. See also Maria Lugones, *Pilgrimages = Peregrinajes: Theorizing Coalition against Multiple Oppressions* (Lanham, MD: Rowman & Littlefield, 2003).

In this section on theorizing intersectionality, I have singled out noteworthy US women of color and their ideas. Let us now turn to women of color feminists on the global stage. Variously known as third-world feminists, postcolonial feminists, and transnational feminists, these feminists highlighted the impact of global capitalism, racism, war, genocide, colonization, and poverty in the experiences of indigenous third-world women.[39] As I mentioned at the start of this essay, postcolonial criticism looks at relations between colonizer and colonized and the ideologies that keep the conquerors and the natives in their respective places. As an entrée into this significant field of feminist theorizing, let's consider one of the most noteworthy essays of postcolonial feminism, Chandra Talpade Mohanty's "Under Western Eyes: Feminist Scholarship and Colonial Discourses."[40] Mohanty's aim was to make visible and dismantle the privilege and ethnocentrism in the discourses of many Western feminists when they write about women living in the third world. She argued that these feminists discursively colonized the historical and material diversities of the lives of real women in the third world, producing a singular monolithic subject, "the third-world woman":

> This average third world woman leads an essentially truncated life based on her feminine gender (read: sexually constrained) and her being "third world" (read: ignorant, poor, uneducated, tradition-bound, domestic, family-oriented, victimized, etc.). This, I suggest, is in contrast to the (implicit) self-representation of Western women as educated, as modern, as having control over their own bodies and sexualities, and the freedom to make their own decisions.[41]

This ideological social construction of the third-world woman in certain feminist discourses was mistaken for real, historical groups of third-world women, reducing them to powerless, victimized, exploited, and sexually oppressed beings. In this discursive reduction, Mohanty located the "colonialist move." The "subject" of these studies was supposed to be about third-world women, but it was

---

39. Tong, *Feminist Thought*, 231–54; Mann, *Doing Feminist Theory*, 355–99.

40. Chandra Talpade Mohanty, "Under Western Eyes: Feminist Scholarship and Colonial Discourses," in *Third World Women and the Politics of Feminism*, ed. Chandra Talpade Mohanty, Ann Russo, and Lourdes Torres (Bloomington: Indiana University Press, 1991), 51–80. First published in 1984. Mohanty revisited this landmark essay sixteen years later in Chandra Talpade Mohanty, "'Under Western Eyes' Revisited: Feminist Solidarity through Anticapitalist Struggles," in *Feminism without Borders: Decolonizing Theory, Practicing Solidarity* (Durham, NC: Duke University Press, 2003), 221–51.

41. Mohanty, "Under Western Eyes: Feminist Scholarship and Colonial Discourses," 56.

really about Western white women and their own ideological self-presentation. The discursive colonization of third-world women, lumping their many differences and specificities in class and ethnicities into the category of average third-world female Other, robbed them of their historical and political agency. They were never able to rise above their status of "object."[42] The purpose of her essay was to make this discursive colonization of the feminist scholarship of her time visible and "decolonize" it.

BECOMING VISIBLE, RECOGNIZING DIFFERENCES, RAISING VOICES

Although we have only seen the tip of the iceberg regarding feminist/intersectional theorizing, we are in a better position to understand its development and observe its connections with feminist biblical scholarship. In the usual histories of second-wave feminism, the focus was primarily on the visibility of (white) women and the notion of gender. Liberal feminism highlighted the rights of women in the political sphere. The emphasis was on the equality of women with men. In contrast, radical feminists argued that women's oppression was enmeshed in a deeper system of male dominance and would not be eliminated simply by laws or the education of women. For them, gender was a social construction apart from biological sex, and based on how they understood that construction of gender, they offered different theories to combat women's oppression by men.

Marxist feminists added class exploitation to women's oppression. They were particularly important in developing standpoint theory and epistemologies to feminist theorizing: the acknowledgment that one could never be neutrally located, that one must continually be aware of how social, historical, and cultural process are constructing us, our thoughts, and our production of knowledge. Knowledge was always produced from someone's or a group's "standpoint." Postmodern feminism took a radically different approach by combining the production of knowledge with power. What we "know" of the world was primarily through different discourses, such as medical, legal, scientific, religious, and so forth, which were controlled by different regimes of power. Maleness or femaleness did not exist outside of these discourses. Later, queer theorizing

---

42. Mohanty, "Under Western Eyes: Feminist Scholarship and Colonial Discourses," 71.

elaborated this discursive understanding of gender further to argue that gender was primarily a performance, a stylized repetition of acts.

Unfortunately, the feminism in the typical histories of the second wave was primarily white-led, marginalizing the activism and standpoints of women of color. The common notion in these histories was that women of color emerged in reaction to and therefore later than white feminism. However, as we have seen in this overview, this would be a mistake. Women of color—African, Latina, Asian American—have been involved in feminist, anti-racist work since the 1970s, raising their distinctive voices in their many-faceted theorizing.[43] As Audre Lorde pointed out, it was not the differences that separated women, but the refusal to recognize those differences.[44] Women of color in varying ways diagnosed and theorized the interconnections of gender, race, class, and sexuality. They developed more complex theories of women's oppression that went beyond the simplistic oppressor/oppressed models by considering not only gender, race, and class as categories of analysis, but also their locations in different domains of power. Finally, we became acquainted with an important postcolonial, transnational feminist, Chandra Mohanty, who took white feminism to task for its ideological construction of the typical "third-world woman." This construction reduced the historical material lives of real third-world women to the status of victims, stripping them of their historical and political agency.

In various ways, through feminist theorizing and activism, white feminists and feminists of color were able to make their voices heard and challenge deeply sexist, racist, hierarchical, and heteronormative systems of male dominance. And they continue to do so. Feminist biblical scholars were and continue to be indebted to them.

FEMINIST PERSPECTIVES ON
THE HEBREW BIBLE

EARLY MILESTONES

Created as the first woman who supposedly tempted man to sin, which led to his and humanity's "fall," the character of Eve in Genesis 1–3 became the flashpoint not only for scores of misogynous

---

43. Thompson, "Multiracial Feminism," 51–56.
44. See fn 26 above.

interpretations but also for early feminist ones. Twelfth-century German abbess Hildegard of Bingen saw Eve as prefiguring Mary, the mother of Jesus. Before the fall, sex between her and Adam was free of lust, their relationship complementary and interdependent. She would give birth painlessly through her side in the manner that she was created from Adam.[45] Christine de Pizan later argued that Eve, created from Adam's rib, would therefore "stand by his side as companion and never lie at his feet like a slave, and also that he would love her as his own flesh" (*The Book of the City of Ladies*, 1405). Pizan asserted that Eve was created in God's image, even surpassing Adam, who was created from the ground, because she was created from Adam's very substance, "the noblest substance which had ever been created."[46] Through the voice of Pilate's wife, who warned her husband to have "nothing to do with that just man," Jesus (Matt 27:19), Amelia Lanyer gave a spirited defense of Eve in *Salve Deus Rex Judaeorum* (1611). Though her fault was great, Adam was the one to be most blamed, because he should have refused the serpent, being of greater strength and the one who actually received God's command about the fruit. If Eve stumbled, it was for the knowledge the fruit could give her and her spouse:

> If Eve did err, it was for knowledge' sake,
> The fruit being fair persuaded him to fall:
>   No subtle Serpent's falsehood did betray him,
>   If he would eat it, who had power to stay him?
> Not Eve, whose fault was only too much love,
> Which made her give this present to her Dear,
> That what she tasted, he likewise might prove,
> Whereby his knowledge might become more clear.[47]

During the nineteenth-century, two US feminist interpreters of note, one white and one African American, presented their insights on the first woman. Both were involved in the abolitionist and the women's suffrage movements of the time. Elizabeth Cady Stanton assembled a committee of learned (white) women to publish *The Woman's Bible*, to provide commentaries on those portions of the Bible that dealt

---

45. Cited in Gerda Lerner, "One Thousand Years of Feminist Bible Criticism," in *The Creation of Feminist Consciousness: From the Middle Ages to Eighteen-Seventy*, Women and History (New York: Oxford University Press, 1993), 142–43.

46. Lerner, *The Creation of Feminist Consciousness*, 144–45.

47. Amelia Lanyer, "Eve's Apology in Defense of Women," in *Salve Deus Rex Judæorum*, 1611, CharlesYoungs.com, https://tinyurl.com/y7xhvtpq.

with women. "Whatever the Bible may be made to do in Hebrew or Greek, in plain English it does not exalt and dignify women."[48] Her characterization of Eve before the serpent in Genesis 3 would resonate with one of the first feminist biblical scholars, Phyllis Trible, more than eighty years later:

> In this prolonged interview, the unprejudiced reader must be impressed with the courage, the dignity, and the lofty ambition of the woman. The tempter evidently had a profound knowledge of human nature, and saw at a glance the high character of the person he met by chance in his walks in the garden. He did not try to tempt her from the path of duty by brilliant jewels, rich dresses, worldly luxuries or pleasures, but with the promise of knowledge, with the wisdom of the Gods.[49]

One of thirteen children, Sojourner Truth (née Isabella Baumfree) was born a slave in a Dutch colony, speaking Dutch until she was eleven when her abusive new master forced her to use English. She was sold to two more masters until she was freed on July 4, 1827, by the New York legislature along with all the other slaves in the state. A traveling evangelist, she eventually added abolition and women's suffrage to her sermons. At the Women's Rights Convention in Akron, Ohio, she delivered her famous "Ain't I a Woman?" speech in 1851:

> That man over there says that women need to be helped into carriages, and lifted over ditches, and to have the best place everywhere. Nobody ever helps me into carriages, or over mud puddles or gives me any best place and ain't I a woman? Look at me! Look at my arm! I have plowed, and planted, and gathered into barns, and no man could head me—and ain't I a woman? I could work as much and eat as much as a man (when I could get it), and bear the lash as well—and ain't I a woman? I have borne thirteen children and seen them almost all sold off into slavery, and when I cried out with a mother's grief, none but Jesus heard—and ain't I a woman?

She concluded this famous speech with a reference to Eve.

> If the first woman God ever made was strong enough to turn the world upside down, all alone, these together ought to be able to turn it back

---

48. Elizabeth Cady Stanton, *The Woman's Bible* (Boston: Northeastern University Press, 1993), 12. First published 1895.
49. Stanton, *The Woman's Bible*, 24.

and get it right side up again; and now they are asking to do it, the men better let them.[50]

If one woman could upset the world order, the women assembled in Akron could make it right again. She enjoined the men to let the convention get on with the business of women's suffrage and support them in this endeavor.[51]

FEMINIST LITERARY AND HISTORICAL
INTERPRETATIONS OF THE BIBLE

Because of the profusion of feminist biblical scholarship since the 1970s, the following survey is necessarily selective, highlighting some of the major moments in feminist and intersectional analyses of the Hebrew Bible. This first section considers those feminist biblical studies that mainly apply the literary and historical methods of the biblical guild.

The biblical studies guild is very diverse in the traditional methods used to analyze a difficult text that was composed over a long period of time, in different languages, in several geographical areas, and often under and in response to many domestic and international conflicts. Methods, such as source, form, redaction, and sociological criticism, regard the Bible as a historical text, examining the different historical, social, and cultural Israelite and ancient Near Eastern contexts in which the texts were written and edited. In contrast, methods such as narrative criticism, rhetorical criticism, poetics, and reader response criticism primarily study the Bible as a literary text and the significant rhetorical features of its prose and poetic genres. Literary criticism of the Bible particularly emerged during the 1970s in reaction to the dominance of the historical-critical methods up to that point.[52]

The historical and literary criticisms reveal that the Hebrew Bible

50. "Sojourner Truth: Ar'n't I a Woman?, 1851 (1797–1883)," in *Ripples of Hope: Great American Civil Rights Speeches*, ed. Josh Gottheimer, Bill Clinton, and Mary Frances Berry (New York: Basic Civitas, 2003); Karen Baker-Fletcher, "Anna Julia Cooper and Sojourner Truth: Two Nineteenth-Century Black Feminist Interpreters of Scripture," in *Search the Scriptures: A Feminist Introduction*, ed. Elisabeth Schüssler Fiorenza (New York: Crossroad, 1995), 41–51.

51. For other nineteenth-century women writers on Eve, see Marion Ann Taylor and Heather E. Weir, eds., *Let Her Speak for Herself: Nineteenth-Century Women Writing on Women in Genesis* (Waco, TX: Baylor University Press, 2006), 21–105.

52. For an introduction to different methods of biblical interpretation, see Corrine Carvalho, *Primer on Biblical Methods* (Winona, MN: Anselm Academic, 2009); see also Joel M. LeMon and

is mainly the work of elite men. Although they were only a tiny minority of the population of ancient Israel, their upper-class male sociohistorical and religious imprints are dominant and normative throughout the text. Furthermore, biblical scholars and religious interpreters of the bible, such as clergy, have primarily been male. Thus the composition of the biblical text as well as its interpretation throughout the ages tends to focus on male interests and ideologies. This changed during the 1970s and '80s, when professionally trained female biblicists began to apply feminist perspectives in their historical and literary exegesis (interpretation) of the Hebrew Bible.[53] Just as there are a plurality of exegetical methods employed in the study of the biblical text, so too will these feminist biblical scholars adopt diverse literary and historical toolboxes to analyze the male-centeredness of the Hebrew Bible and its interpretation.[54]

We saw in the discussion above that the radical feminists criticized the "rights" focus of the liberal feminists by insisting that women's oppression would not simply be eliminated by equal educational or legal opportunities. It went much deeper because it was embedded in a male system characterized by power, dominance, hierarchy, and competition that was often called patriarchy. Recognizing patriarchy in the Hebrew Bible, Phyllis Trible argues for "Depatriarchalizing in Biblical Interpretation," in one of the first essays of feminist biblical interpretation, although she does not label herself a radical feminist.[55] Trible does not perceive an either/or opposition between biblical faith and the movement of women's liberation. As a Christian believer, she maintains that the objective of biblical faith was not to create or perpetuate patriarchy but rather assist in the salvation of both women and men. The biblical text itself contains the means of depatriarchalizing its sexism in, for example, the maternal imagery for the deity, the Song of Songs, and the Exodus tradition. However, because male biases of the translator and interpreter amplify the

Kent H. Richards, eds., *Method Matters: Essays on the Interpretation of the Hebrew Bible in Honor of David L. Petersen*, Resources for Biblical Study (Atlanta: Society of Biblical Literature, 2009).

53. For a nuanced overview of feminist and intersectional biblical interpretation, see Nyasha Junior, *An Introduction to Womanist Biblical Interpretation* (Louisville: Westminster John Knox, 2015), 76–121.

54. For an anthology devoted to the various methods employed by feminist biblical scholars, see Susanne Scholz, ed., *Feminist Interpretation of the Hebrew Bible in Retrospect: Volume 3: Methods*, Recent Research in Biblical Studies 9 (Sheffield: Sheffield Phoenix, 2016).

55. Phyllis Trible, "Depatriarchalizing in Biblical Interpretation," *Journal of the American Academy of Religion* 41 (1973): 30–48.

sexism of the text, a feminist hermeneutic must be applied to counteract them.

Applying a careful literary reading of the Hebrew, Trible reinterprets the person of Eve in her classic work, *God and the Rhetoric of Sexuality*.[56] Rather than being the cunning temptress whose sole purpose was simply as man's helpmate, Eve's creation becomes the highpoint in Genesis 2, resulting in the creation of sexuality itself. Instead of a subservient helper, she becomes the man's companion. Trible's rehabilitation of Eve, as an intelligent, theological interpreter of God's command when confronting the snake (Genesis 3), is similar to Elizabeth Cady's Stanton's assessment of Eve in *The Woman's Bible Commentary*, cited previously.

In the companion volume to this classic book, Trible deals with the male violence against women in the Hebrew Bible directly in *Texts of Terror: Literary-Feminist Readings of Biblical Narratives*. She singles out four stories of the cruelty men inflict upon women: Hagar, the cast-off Egyptian slave woman (Genesis 16 and 21); Tamar, the Judean princess raped by her half-brother (2 Samuel 13); the concubine from Bethlehem, dismembered by her husband after being gang-raped (Judges 19); Jephthah's daughter, sacrificed as a burnt offering by her father (Judges 11).[57] Usually not read or preached in churches and synagogues, these stories are "texts of terror" for women. Trible enjoins the reader to hold these neglected women "*in memoriam*," by interpreting these "stories of outrage on behalf of their female victims in order to recover a neglected history, to remember a past that the present embodies, and to pray that these terrors shall not come to pass again. In telling sad stories, a feminist hermeneutic seeks to redeem the time."[58]

Other significant feminist scholars of the 1970–1980s adopt historical approaches to the biblical text. In her pioneering essay, "Images of Women in the Old Testament," Phyllis Bird attempts to deal with the diversity of these images by situating them in the historical times in which they were composed and in the literary genres, such as law codes, in which they are found. For example, these laws disclose the place of women in Israelite notions of family

---

56. Phyllis Trible, *God and the Rhetoric of Sexuality* (Philadelphia: Fortress Press, 1978), 72–143.

57. Phyllis Trible, *Texts of Terror: Literary-Feminist Readings of Biblical Narratives* (Philadelphia: Fortress Press, 1984).

58. Trible, *Texts of Terror*, 3.

and kinship, sexuality and its transgressions, where she was "a legal non-person; where she did become visible it was as a dependent, and usually an inferior, in a male-centered and male-dominated society."[59] Bird's historical work on women's place in Israelite cult reveals that the centralization of Israelite cult restricted women's participation in pilgrim feasts and local shrines. However, cross-cultural studies draw attention to rituals and devotions revered by women, especially in the different cycles of their lives, which may have been hidden beneath the biblical text or regarded as frivolous or heterodox by the dominant male cult.[60]

Carol Meyers enlists archeology and the social sciences to reconstruct the lives of ancient Israelite women, particularly during Israel's pre-monarchic or tribal period. Anthropological studies of pre-industrial societies demonstrate that even though women have been denied access to formal avenues of power, they can exert informal power to achieve their ends. Meyers argues that the focus on subsistence living in the pre-monarchic period rendered women and their roles to be pivotal for the survival of the agrarian family household. Women controlled food preparation and resources; they were involved in subsistence crafts, such as making pottery, tools, and clothing; they had a crucial role in the religious, moral, and social education of young children. "In short, female power will be as significant as male power, and perhaps even greater."[61]

Athalya Brenner's The Israelite Woman is the first book-length treatment of women's professions and social institutions, such as queens, wise women, poets, prophets, magicians, sorcerers, witches, and prostitutes, and the different literary types of women and their behaviors, as mothers, temptresses, foreigners, and ancestresses.[62] In the second edition of this book thirty years later, Brenner relates how she was turned down for tenure at Haifa University because

59. Phyllis A. Bird, "Images of Women in the Old Testament," in Religion and Sexism: Images of Woman in the Jewish and Christian Traditions, ed. Rosemary Radford Ruether (New York: Simon & Schuster, 1974), 56.

60. Phyllis Bird, "The Place of Women in the Israelite Cultus," in Ancient Israelite Religion: Essays in Honor of Frank Moore Cross, ed. Patrick D. Miller, Paul D. Hanson, and S. Dean McBride (Philadelphia: Fortress Press, 1987), 397–419.

61. Carol Meyers, Discovering Eve: Ancient Israelite Women in Context (New York: Oxford University Press, 1988), 176; Meyers considerably updated this book in Carol Meyers, Rediscovering Eve: Ancient Israelite Women in Context (New York: Oxford University Press, 2013).

62. Athalya Brenner, The Israelite Woman: Social Role and Literary Type in Biblical Narrative (Sheffield: JSOT Press, 1985).

of this book, since her committee felt that "feminist research was not truly academic, not meaningful, a passing fad and waste of time and energy and money, and that its practitioners in any field should be excised from the guild."[63] Devastated, especially after losing her appeal, Brenner began working on one of the most influential volumes of feminist biblical criticism, *The Feminist Companion to the Hebrew Bible* (series 1 and 2, 1993–2001). For the different books of the Hebrew Bible, she brought together previously published articles, but primarily new ones on the expanding and diverse literature on feminist biblical interpretation.

The 1980s also witnessed the publication of several essay collections that highlight the diversity of feminist literary and historical approaches to the biblical text. These include the papers from the 1980 session on "The Effects of Women's Studies on Biblical Studies" during the centennial celebrations for the Society of Biblical Literature;[64] a *Semeia* volume on "The Bible and Feminist Hermeneutics," edited by New Testament scholar Mary Ann Tolbert;[65] *Feminist Perspectives on Biblical Scholarship*, edited by New Testament scholar Adela Yarbro Collins;[66] and *Feminist Interpretation of the Bible*, edited by theologian Letty Russell.[67]

Perhaps the highpoint of feminist scholarship during the 1990s was the publication of *The Women's Bible Commentary* in 1992.[68] In contrast to Cady Stanton's *The Woman's Bible*, professionally trained female scholars penned the commentaries for each book of the Old and New Testaments, selecting those passages that they judged to be of particular relevance to women. The change in nomenclature from Stanton's "Woman's Bible" to "Women's Bible" reflects the editors' recognition of the diversity among women who read and study it. A second edition of the commentary was published in 1998, adding commentaries for each book of the Apocrypha or deuterocanonical

---

63. Athalya Brenner-Idan, *The Israelite Woman: Social Role and Literary Type in Biblical Narrative*, 2nd ed., Cornerstones (London: Bloomsbury, 2015), xii.

64. See the story behind this centennial in Phyllis Trible, "The Effects of Women's Studies on Biblical Studies: An Introduction," *Journal for the Study of the Old Testament* 7, no. 22 (1982): 3–5.

65. Mary Ann Tolbert, ed., "The Bible and Feminist Hermeneutics," *Semeia* 28 (1983): 3–126.

66. Adela Yarbro Collins, ed., *Feminist Perspectives on Biblical Scholarship* (Chico, CA: Scholars, 1985).

67. Letty M. Russell, ed., *Feminist Interpretation of the Bible* (Philadelphia: Westminster, 1985).

68. Carol A. Newsom and Sharon H. Ringe, eds., *The Women's Bible Commentary* (Louisville: Westminster John Knox, 1992).

books and the addition of a bibliography at the end of the volume to supplement the ones in the original articles. A twentieth-anniversary third edition appeared in 2012, which replaced some articles with those of newer scholars and updated those that remained. Furthermore, this edition examined thirteen female biblical characters in their reinterpretation in art and in other ancient and modern texts.

FEMINIST INTERDISCIPLINARY EXPLORATIONS OF THE BIBLE

Particularly during the 1990s–2000s, feminist biblical scholars began to adopt some of the critical theories and approaches of disciplines beyond the traditional historical and literary methods. These postmodern feminist approaches include deconstructive criticism, Marxist/materialist criticism, gender and queer criticism, and cultural criticism.

We begin first with Esther Fuchs, an Israeli secular Jew, who contributed two essays in one of the earliest collections of feminist biblical scholarship, writing on the sexual politics of mothers and the alleged "deceptiveness" of biblical women.[69] Lamenting that Fuchs was a lone voice crying in the wilderness about the insidious ways in which the biblical text communicates patriarchy, Pamela Milne argued in 1997 that feminist biblical scholarship needed to have greater connections and interactions with the larger feminist movement and feminist scholarship in other disciplines.[70] Fuchs is significant because she is one of the few feminist biblical scholars who directly engage the daunting field of postmodern feminist theory in her writings.[71] Fuchs is critical of what she calls a "resurgence of neoliberal feminist recuperations of the Hebrew Bible" in the 1990s–2000s. Recall in the discussion in the first section of this chapter that liberal feminism tries to convince women that they could

69. Esther Fuchs, "The Literary Characterization of Mothers and Sexual Politics in the Hebrew Bible," and "Who Is Hiding the Truth? Deceptive Women and Biblical Androcentrism," in *Feminist Perspectives on Biblical Scholars*, ed. Adela Yarbro Collins (Chico, CA: Scholars, 1985), 117–36, 137–44.

70. Pamela J. Milne, "Toward Feminist Companionship: The Future of Feminist Biblical Studies and Feminism," in *A Feminist Companion to Reading the Bible: Approaches, Methods and Strategies*, ed. Athalya Brenner and Carole Fontaine (Sheffield: Sheffield Academic, 1997), 39–60.

71. Along with her critical survey of feminist theory, several of her important essays are reprinted in Esther Fuchs, *Feminist Theory and the Bible*, Feminist Studies and Sacred Texts (Lanham, MD: Lexington, 2016).

be and should be like men in order to win access to the public sphere and civil rights, highlighting equality with men, encouraging liberal ideals for women, such as independence, rationalism, individualism, and influence. Fuchs's analysis reveals how several feminist biblical scholars impose neoliberal idealizations of strength, assertiveness, self-determination, and independence upon biblical women, such as Miriam, Deborah, Jael, Abigail, and Delilah, without recognizing the male ideological and political framing of their stories.

> By ignoring or denying the analytical prisms of ideology, gender as power, and discourse—the important interventions of Marxist, radical, and poststructuralist feminisms—neoliberal feminist approaches return us to the traditional myth of the "feminine mystique"—to typologies and representations of sexual difference that continue to inform Western culture.[72]

Fuchs acknowledges that seeking feminist models in biblical women is understandable, "but in the process of this quest we must make sure not to project narrow and largely discarded definitions of feminism on what are ultimately patriarchal constructs."[73]

Firmly ensconced in postmodern theories of language, deconstructive criticism is an act of reading that exposes the ways in which biblical texts contradict themselves and highlights elements of the text that traditional readings have overlooked or have intentionally ignored. Such a reading explores the complex and sometimes conflictual nature in the text's production of meaning, as opposed to a reading that reduces a text's meaning to a single or dominant interpretation.[74] Important feminist biblical scholars employing deconstructive criticism include Danna Nolan Fewell,[75]

---

72. Esther Fuchs, "Reclaiming the Hebrew Bible for Women: The Neoliberal Turn in Contemporary Feminist Scholarship," *Journal of Feminist Studies in Religion* 24, no. 2 (2008): 63–64.

73. Fuchs, "Reclaiming the Hebrew Bible for Women," 65.

74. Gale A. Yee, ed., *Judges and Method: New Approaches in Biblical Studies*, 2nd ed. (Minneapolis: Fortress Press, 2007), 238.

75. Danna Nolan Fewell and David M. Gunn, *Gender, Power, and Promise: The Subject of the Bible's First Story* (Nashville: Abingdon, 1993). For a discussion of the presuppositions and application of the method, see Danna Nolan Fewell, "Deconstructive Criticism: Achsah and the (E)razed City of Writing," in *Judges and Method: New Approaches in Biblical Studies*, ed. Gale A. Yee (Minneapolis: Fortress Press, 2007), 113–37.

Mieke Bal,[76] and Yvonne Sherwood.[77] In an accessible example of deconstructive analysis, Danna Fewell contrasts two feminist readings of the book of Ruth. Phyllis Trible produces a positive or text-affirming reading of the book, while on the opposite end of the spectrum, Esther Fuchs represents a negative or text-resistant one. Fewell argues that both scholars omitted those elements that did not accord with their thesis, and therefore one must constantly reread. Any reading that results in a text that is thematically unified is a misreading, because the text itself contains the seeds of its own contradiction. She then applies deconstruction in an analysis of Esther 1, the story of Queen Vashti's banishment for her disobedience to her husband, to expose the fragility of male sovereignty in a story utterly soaked in patriarchy.[78]

Marxist/materialist criticism investigates the socioeconomic class relations in the biblical texts, such as rich and poor, elite and peasant, royal court and landowners, empire and vassal state, and so forth. Feminist biblical scholars adopting such criticism incorporate the issues surrounding gender into their class analysis.[79] For example, applying the standpoint theory of Marxist feminism, Avaren Ipsen analyzes the stories of biblical prostitutes, such as the Canaanite Rahab (Joshua 2 and 6), the prostitutes before Solomon (1 Kings 3), and the whore of Babylon (Revelation 17–19) with a racially mixed reading group of activist sex workers in Berkeley, California (SWOP, the Sex Worker Outreach Project). Standpoint theory presumes that the women who do sex work have important subjugated knowledge that deserves theoretical articulation, producing thought-provoking results when undertaken within the discipline of biblical interpretation. Ipsen's sex workers highlight the systemic economic circumstances of their trade: No young girls grow up wanting to be a prostitutes, but they become prostitutes because they are poor,

---

76. Mieke Bal, *Lethal Love: Feminist Literary Readings of Biblical Love Stories* (Bloomington: Indiana University Press, 1987); Mieke Bal, *Murder and Difference: Gender, Genre, and Scholarship on Sisera's Death* (Bloomington: Indiana University Press, 1988); Mieke Bal, *Death and Dissymmetry: The Politics of Coherence in the Book of Judges* (Chicago: University of Chicago Press, 1988).

77. Yvonne Sherwood, *The Prostitute and the Prophet: Hosea's Marriage in Literary-Theoretical Perspective* (Sheffield: Sheffield Academic, 1996).

78. Danna Nolan Fewell, "Feminist Reading of the Hebrew Bible: Affirmation, Resistance and Transformation," *JSOT* 39 (1987): 77–87.

79. Gale A. Yee, *Poor Banished Children of Eve: Woman as Evil in the Hebrew Bible* (Minneapolis: Fortress Press, 2003); Roland Boer and Jorunn Økland, eds., *Marxist Feminist Criticism of the Bible* (Sheffield: Sheffield Phoenix, 2008).

starving, and need to feed their families. They are quick to deduce Rahab's anxiety with the king's officers of Jericho, because they are often squeezed for information or blackmailed for sexual favors by the police. In the story of the prostitutes before Solomon, they highlight from their own daily experiences the violence of Solomon's courtroom, the corruption of the court system itself, and that a prostitute's testimony is always questionable. Avoiding the usual characterizations of the two prostitutes as the "good" and "bad" mother, the SWOP activists sympathize with both from their own personal experiences of motherhood in their sex work. Ipsen hopes that these readings will inform the field of biblical studies, while empowering the liberation struggles of sex workers, whose population "has dramatically increased in the current neo-liberal global economy where poverty and the feminization of poverty is ubiquitous."[80]

Gender criticism is an approach to reading that explores the role of gender in society and cultural products, while simultaneously revealing the instability of categories and norms associated with gender, such as "man" and "woman," "masculine" and "feminine."[81] Along with feminist theory, gender criticism includes insights from queer theory, masculinity studies, and intersectional analyses. In a provocatively titled article, "From Gender Reversal to Genderfuck," Deryn Guest applies gender criticism to the story of the assassin Jael in Judges 4–5, revealing one of the hallmarks of gender criticism, the volatility of the gender binary.[82] Guest rejects interpretations of Jael that persist in confining gender to the binaries male/female, masculine/feminine. As long as scholars remain within this closed dichotomous system, Jael's transgressive acts will only be seen as gender "reversal" that for Guest simply shifts the ground from one gender to the other. According to Guest, all commentators have not been able to break through the male/female binary in consistently referring to Jael as female, because they fail to see, à la Judith Butler, that gender is a performance. Guest prefers instead to resist, subvert,

80. Avaren E. Ipsen, *Sex Working and the Bible* (London: Equinox, 2009), 11.

81. Ken Stone, "Gender Criticism: The Un-Manning of Abimelech," in *Judges and Method: New Approaches in Biblical Studies*, ed. Gale A. Yee (Minneapolis: Fortress Press, 2007), 183–201; and Nicole J. Ruane, "When Women Aren't Enough: Gender Criticism in Feminist Hebrew Bible Interpretation," in *Feminist Interpretation of the Hebrew Bible in Retrospect. Vol. 3: Methods*, ed. Susanne Scholz (Sheffield: Sheffield Phoenix, 2016), 243–60.

82. Deryn Guest, "From Gender Reversal to Genderfuck: Reading Jael through a Lesbian Lens," in *Bible Trouble: Queer Reading at the Boundaries of Biblical Scholarship*, ed. Teresa J. Hornsby and Ken Stone (Atlanta: Society of Biblical Literature, 2011), 9–43.

undo, and deconstruct these binaries to reveal them as social constructions. While several scholars have described Jael's violent assassination of Sisera with a phallic tent peg as a reversal of male rape, Guest maintains that

> Jael is not a *woman* warrior and equally Jael is not a *male* rapist. The narrator has conjured a figure who carries a resonance he could probably never have anticipated for readers in the early twenty-first century. Jael is a figure who unsettles and destabilizes, whose performativity provides one of those unintelligible genders that give the lie to ideas of sex as abiding substance.[83]

It is this gender blur and confusion of Jael as "not-woman/not-man" that aggravates and provokes the dominant structures of patriarchy in the Jael narrative.[84]

Cultural criticism explores the different ways in which the Bible has been received and interpreted in the different high and popular cultures that encounter it. It investigates Scripture's history of reception in its various duplications from very early times all the way up to the present.[85] Perhaps the most memorable introduction of feminist cultural studies to the biblical guild is J. Cheryl Exum's presentation, "Bathsheba Plotted, Shot, and Painted," at the 1994 session of the Society of Biblical Literature. Comparing 2 Samuel 11 with different paintings and movie versions of David and Bathsheba's adulterous encounter, Exum demonstrates how the different media used by painters and film directors focus on Bathsheba's body as an object of sexual desire and male aggression. "Since the essay self-consciously looks at looking, I invite its readers to join me in looking at our own gaze—at our collusion, or complicity, or resistance when faced with the exposure of female flesh for our literary or visual consumption."[86] Feminist cultural studies on the Bible has been

---

83. Guest, "From Gender Reversal to Genderfuck," 26. Emphasis in orginal.

84. Guest pushes the disciplinary boundaries of feminist biblical criticism to argue for "genderqueer" readings of the Bible in Deryn Guest, *Beyond Feminist Biblical Studies*, The Bible in the Modern World 47 (Sheffield: Sheffield Phoenix, 2012).

85. Gale A. Yee, ""What Is Cultural Criticism of the Old Testament?," in *Why Read the Old Testament? Questions Asked and Unasked: The Legacy of Fr. Lawrence Boadt*, ed. Corrine L. Carvalho (Mahwah, NJ: Paulist, 2013), 43–55; David M. Gunn, "Cultural Criticism: Viewing the Sacrifice of Jephthah's Daughter," in *Judges and Method: New Approaches in Biblical Studies*, ed. Gale A. Yee (Minneapolis: Fortress Press, 2007), 202–36.

86. Published in J. Cheryl Exum, "Bathsheba Plotted, Shot, and Painted," *Semeia* 74 (1996): 47; also J. Cheryl Exum, *Plotted, Shot, and Painted: Cultural Representations of Biblical Women* (Sheffield: Sheffield Academic, 1996), where she examines Michal, Ruth and Naomi, and Delilah.

applied to the persons Adam and Eve,[87] to Hollywood films,[88] religion, politics, the media,[89] and advertising.[90]

INTERSECTIONAL PERSPECTIVES ON
THE HEBREW BIBLE

Just as feminists of color were active in the beginnings of the US women's movement in the 1960s, so too have feminists of color been involved in feminist biblical studies since its initial stages. Feminist biblical scholars of color bring their different racial/ethnic and class locations in a dominant white society to bear on the interpretation of the biblical text, using an array of exegetical methods and approaches. This short survey will primarily discuss African American, Asian American, and postcolonial feminist biblical scholars of the Hebrew Bible.

Among female African American biblical scholars, how they identify themselves as "feminist" in their racial locations is an important consideration. African American women have historically been reticent to adopt the identification of "feminist" for themselves because of the racism they see in white feminism. One of the early black feminist theorists, bell hooks, avoids saying "I am a feminist" by using the descriptive "I advocate feminism." For her, this response implies a choice to be committed to the feminist struggle, which she sees as a movement to end sexist oppression, while being open to supporting other political movements as well.[91] Other African American women embrace the term "womanist," coined by Alice Walker in 1983, which designates "a black feminist or feminist of color" at its first level.[92] Still others prefer the nomenclature of "black feminist," acknowledging the contributions of a generation of black feminist foremothers, which the term womanist may preclude.[93]

---

87. Linda S. Schearing and Valarie H. Ziegler, *Enticed by Eden: How Western Culture Uses, Confuses, (and Sometimes Abuses) Adam and Eve* (Waco, TX: Baylor University Press, 2013).

88. Alice Bach, ed., "Biblical Glamour and Hollywood Glitz," *Semeia* 74 (1996): 1–214.

89. Alice Bach, *Religion, Politics, Media in the Broadband Era* (Sheffield: Sheffield Phoenix, 2004).

90. Katie B. Edwards, *Admen and Eve: The Bible in Contemporary Advertising* (Sheffield: Sheffield Phoenix, 2012).

91. hooks, *Feminist Theory: From Margin to Center*, 29.

92. Alice Walker, *In Search of Our Mothers' Gardens* (Orlando, FL: Harcourt, 1983), xi–xii. Walker's inclusion of "a woman who loves other women, sexually and/or nonsexually" in her second part of the definition will be offensive to some black church women.

93. Traci C. West, "Is a Womanist a Black Feminist? Marking the Distinctions and Defying

Nyasha Junior, author of a recent introduction to womanist biblical interpretation, does not label herself as either a feminist or a womanist, because neither term conveys who she is professionally.[94] The latest collection of African American female biblical scholars is explicitly titled *Womanist Interpretations of the Bible*, even though some of its contributors self-identify differently.[95] Acknowledging this complexity, I will refer to the identification of African American scholars with the terms they use for themselves. For example, Wil Gafney offers a fluid self-definition, depending upon her racial/ethnic context:

> My own practice of self-definition varies according to context. Like hooks and Dube my primary self-designation is as a black feminist. I am a black feminist who works and worships in solidarity with my womanist sisters. My location in feminist, rather than womanist, space reflects my intent to participate in the redemption of a radically egalitarian ethic from the pale hands of those who infected it with racism and classism. But in environments in which the radically egalitarian ideals of feminism have been hijacked by racism and classism, I self-identity as a womanist to avoid being coopted by white feminists. Occasionally my experience of my hybridized identity results in a hybridized identifier, fem/womanist, which stands at the intersection of feminist and womanist practices.[96]

Renita J. Weems was the first African American woman to earn a PhD in Hebrew Bible, in 1989 at Princeton Theological Seminary. While not an academic monograph, her cross-over book for African American Christian women, *Just a Sister Away*, is considered the first womanist biblical interpretation, since she employs "some of the best fruits of feminist biblical criticism, along with the best of the Afro-American oral tradition, with its gifts for story-telling and its love of dramas."[97] Her chapters deal with female pairs, such as Hagar

Them: A Black Feminist Response," in *Deeper Shades of Purple: Womanism in Religion and Society*, ed. Stacey M. Floyd-Thomas (New York: New York University Press, 2006), 291–95.

94. Junior, *An Introduction to Womanist Biblical Interpretation*, xxi.

95. Gay L. Byron and Vanessa Lovelace, eds., *Womanist Interpretations of the Bible: Expanding the Discourse*, Semeia Studies, 85 (Atlanta: Society of Biblical Literature, 2016).

96. Wilda C. M. Gafney, "A Black Feminist Approach to Biblical Studies," *Encounter* 67, no. 4 (2006): 397. Adopting and modernizing a rabbinic exegetical commentary, Gafney develops a "womanist midrash," not only in several articles but most recently a book on well- and lesser-known women in the Hebrew Bible (*Womanist Midrash: A Reintroduction to the Women of Torah and the Throne* [Louisville: Westminster John Knox, 2017]).

97. Renita J. Weems, *Just a Sister Away: A Womanist Vision of Women's Relationships in the Bible* (San Diego: Lura Media, 1988), ix.

and Sarah, Naomi and Ruth, Jephthah's daughter and the mourning women, Vashti and Esther, Lot's wife and her daughters. Analyzing these characters through the lenses of gender, race, and class, she connects their stories to present-day experiences of African American women.

Weems's article, "Gomer: Victim of Violence or Victim of Metaphor," foregrounds the problematic nature of the marriage metaphor in Hosea 2 to describe the covenantal relationship between God and Israel.[98] She continues to explore its hermeneutical issues, that "it's not just a metaphor," in her monograph *Battered Love: Marriage, Sex, and Violence in the Hebrew Prophets*, concluding:

> Not only does the image of the promiscuous wife have the potential to reinforce violence against women. It also has the potential to exclude whole segments of the population from hearing and responding to the biblical message. It does this by asking women who have been raped and violated or who live with the threat of rape and violation to join with writers in inhabiting a world where women's rape and violation are theological justifiable. On these grounds alone, metaphors require our constant vigilance.[99]

In her contribution to the first essay collection of African American biblical interpretation, "Reading *Her Way* through the Struggle: African American Women and the Bible," Weems tackles the question of why African American women, who are marginalized by gender and ethnicity, and often class, continue to find the Bible meaningful.[100] She argues that because African American culture has primarily been a hearing one, *particular* readings and reading strategies of the text become more important than the text itself. African American women have consistently identified with those passages where the oppressed were freed, the humbled exalted, and the long-suffering rewarded, even though the sexism of the Bible creates some ambivalence in the way they read it. On the one hand, African American women read the Bible to resist what they have been taught about their ineligibility to read, and on the other, to

---

98. Renita J. Weems, "Gomer: Victim of Violence or Victim of Metaphor?" *Semeia* 47 (1989): 87–104.

99. Renita J. Weems, *Battered Love: Marriage, Sex, and Violence in the Hebrew Prophets* (Minneapolis: Fortress Press, 1995), 115–16.

100. Renita J. Weems, "Reading Her Way through the Struggle: African American Women and the Bible," in *Stony the Road We Trod: African American Biblical Interpretation* (Minneapolis: Fortress Press, 1991), 58.

comply in some ways with what they have been taught about how to read it, namely, to identify with the dominant voice against the oppressed, the humbled, the long-suffering. The challenge for African American women is to use whatever means necessary to recover the voice of the oppressed within the biblical texts.[101]

"As a Christian (Protestant) and feminist/womanist African-American female," Cheryl B. Anderson tackles the biblical laws in the book of the covenant and Deuteronomic law, on the ways in which they construct gender ideologically and are inherently violent against women.[102] As a former attorney, she adopts the criteria of feminist legal theorists to make her argument that the law codes do indeed equate masculinity with male dominance.[103] Taking, for example, some of the laws regarding rape in the Hebrew Bible, she argues that the law is male if it systematically favors men and oppresses women, if it is neutral in form but has a disproportionately negative impact on females, and if it embodies only the male experience.[104] For Anderson, all three criteria are present in the biblical law codes. "These laws are clearly male and as such they follow a gender-role pattern that supports and sustains male dominance."[105] Anderson then engages the critical theorists of the Frankfurt School, specifically the work of Theodor Adorno, Max Horkheimer, and Walter Benjamin, to make the argument that these male laws do not just allow violence against women to occur, but that they are forms of violence in and of themselves.

Intersectional connections among gender, race, class, and sexual orientation are particularly evident in Anderson's second book, in which she calls for the development of an inclusive biblical interpretation. Here, she tackles problematic biblical laws from the perspectives of those regarded as the marginalized Other: women, the poor, non-Israelites (foreigners), gays, indigenous folks, and the colonized. Her liberationist readings collectively involve feminist/womanist, queer, and postcolonial methodologies. Because liberationist struggles are often pitted against each other, Anderson

101. Weems, "Reading Her Way through the Struggle," 72–73.

102. Cheryl B. Anderson, *Women, Ideology and Violence: The Construction of Gender in the Book of the Covenant and Deuteronomic Law*, JSOTSup (New York: Continuum, 2004), 19–20.

103. Anderson (*Women, Ideology and Violence*, 78) here relies on Peggy Sanday's contention that in some cultures, male dominance/female subordination is not an inevitable human occurrence.

104. Anderson, *Women, Ideology and Violence*, 80–91.

105. Anderson, *Women, Ideology and Violence*, 91.

declares that transformative change for inclusive communities can only occur when these liberationist groups strategically incorporate the issues of another marginalized population. Her convictions on this matter are worth quoting at length, because they exemplify the interconnectedness of oppressions in Patricia Hill Collins's matrix of domination and the politics of power and empowerment:[106]

> Instead of supporting the dominant condemnation of homosexuality, heterosexual women need to understand that the same underlying rationale for this condemnation supports the subordination of women. Therefore, fighting heterosexism and homophobia should be an integral part of a feminist agenda. Instead of supporting the dominant condemnation of homosexuality, African American church leaders need to understand that the same underlying rationale for this condemnation supports white supremacy, that is, the dominance of white people over people of color. Therefore, their continuing struggle against racism should include the struggle against heterosexism and homophobia. Instead of supporting the dominant condemnation of homosexuality, African church leaders need to understand that the same underlying rationale for this condemnation supports the dominance of the West and its exploitation of Africa's resources. Therefore, any critique of global capitalism as neocolonialism should also address heterosexism and homophobia. Similarly, instead of condemning the homophobia of African and African American communities, leaders in the lesbian/gay/bisexual/transgender (LGBT) communities need to understand that the same underlying rationale for the condemnation of homosexuality supports racism. Therefore, white LGBT leaders have every reason to struggle against racism as part of their own activities.[107]

African American advocacy appears in other ways in Anderson's writings. Her reflections on the intermarriage ban and its exclusionary racial/ethnic policies in Ezra are correlated with the segregationist and anti-miscegenation laws that were used against African Americans, and whose harmful consequences still linger, even though they have been officially abolished.[108] Finally, Anderson is particularly noted for her work on reading the Hebrew Bible in the

106. See pp. 10–11 above.

107. Cheryl B. Anderson, *Ancient Laws and Contemporary Controversies: The Need for Inclusive Biblical Interpretation* (New York: Oxford University Press, 2009), 153.

108. Cheryl B. Anderson, "Reflections in an Interethnic/Racial Era on Interethnic/Racial Marriage in Ezra," in *They Were All Together in One Place? Toward Minority Biblical Criticism*, ed. Randall C. Bailey, Tat-Siong Benny Liew, and Fernando F. Segovia (Atlanta: Society of Biblical Literature, 2009), 119–40.

contexts of the HIV/AIDS pandemic and especially the responses of the African and African American churches.[109]

If one skimmed the titles in the two volumes of collected essays on Asian American biblical interpretation, several overlapping themes stand out: "finding a home," "home as memory, metaphor, and promise," "the politics of identity," "neither here nor there," "liminality," "betwixt and between," "yin/yang is not me," "constructing hybridity and heterogeneity," "boundary and identity," "obscured beginnings."[110] Asian Americans do not fit neatly into the white/black racial binary. Racially, they are neither white nor black, neither here nor there, but betwixt and between. As immigrants or descendants of immigrants, Asian Americans continue to struggle to find their place, home, and belonging in the white dominant society of the US. And attempting to do so, they have to contend with the covert, overt, and virulent racism targeted against them. It is because of this racism that Asian Americans as a minority group in the US have to explicitly address the construction of racial and ethnic identity for survival and empowerment. "The Bible is of particular importance because the exclusion of and discrimination against Asians in the United States have long been enacted in terms of a struggle to protect not only the nation but also Christendom from these racial *and* religious others."[111]

To read through the lenses of the Chinese American experience, Gale A. Yee singles out the book of Ruth, because it conjoins issues of gender, sexuality, race/ethnicity, immigration, nationality, assimilation, and class in fascinating ways that allow different social groups to read their own stories into the multilayered narrative of Ruth and Naomi. For Yee, the person of Ruth the Moabite embodies

109. Cheryl B. Anderson, "Transatlantic Reflections: Contesting the Margins and Transgressing Boundaries in the Age of AIDS," *Journal of Feminist Studies in Religion* 25, no. 2 (September 2009): 103–7; Cheryl B. Anderson, "Biblical Interpretation as Violence: Genesis 19 and Judges 19 in the Context of HIV and AIDS," in *La Violencia and the Hebrew Bible: The Politics and Histories of Biblical Hermeneutics on the American Continent*, ed. Susanne Scholz and Pablo R. Andiñach, Semeia Studies 82 (Atlanta: Society of Biblical Literature, 2016), 121–36; Cheryl B. Anderson, "The Song of Songs: Redeeming Gender Constructions in the Age of AIDS," in *Womanist Interpretations of the Bible: Expanding the Discourse*, ed. Gay L. Byron and Vanessa Lovelace, Semeia Studies 85 (Atlanta: Society of Biblical Literature, 2016), 73–92.

110. Tat-Siong Benny Liew and Gale A. Yee, eds., *The Bible in Asian America*, Semeia 90/91 (Atlanta: Society of Biblical Literature, 2002); Mary F. Foskett and Jeffrey Kah-jin Kuan, eds., *Ways of Being, Ways of Reading: Asian American Biblical Interpretation* (St. Louis: Chalice, 2006).

111. Tat-Siong Benny Liew, "Asian American Biblical Interpretation," in *The Oxford Encyclopedia of Biblical Interpretation*, ed. Steven L. McKenzie, vol. 1 (Oxford: Oxford University Press, 2013), 37 (36–42).

the dialectical stereotype that has plagued Asian Americans as both a model minority and a perpetual foreigner. On the one hand, Ruth is this devoted widow who rejects her homeland to accompany her Jewish mother-in-law to a strange new land, and her faithfulness attracts the man who will become her new husband and provide for her. As the model immigrant, she teaches the Jewish people the true meaning of God's covenantal love. Similarly, set up against blacks and Latino/as, Asian Americans become the model minority, those who work hard, venerate and respect family, and do not rock the boat. On the other hand, just like those who consistently ask even third-generation Asian Americans, "Where are you *really* from?," the book of Ruth never lets the reader forget that she is a perpetual foreigner, a Moabite, one not fully assimilated into the Israelite community, and one who disappears from the story once she gives birth to Naomi's grandson.[112]

Chinese American biblical scholar Lai Ling Elizabeth Ngan develops an Asian American hermeneutics through the story of Hagar in the book of Genesis. She notes that for much of the twentieth century, those who are not white, black, or Hispanic were classified as "others" in US demographic data. It was through the civil rights movement of the sixties that the category of "Asian" or "Asian American" was added to US censuses, recognizing those who trace their ethnic origins to parts of East or South Asia. The labeling or marking of difference is not a neutral or value-free act, because lines and boundaries make some things visible and others invisible. "Since the marking of boundaries and ethnicity is socially constructed, Asian Americans must ask if these boundary markers are valid and whether lines should be drawn differently."[113] Ngan points out that Hagar does not identify herself as an Egyptian, but is marked repeatedly as one from the dominant perspective of the exilic or postexilic storyteller whose own ethnicity serves as the norm of the story. Narrated from his perspective, Hagar's Egyptian identity marks her as belonging to a people who oppressed the Israelites in the land of bondage and slavery. However, for Ngan, Hagar herself redraws

112. Gale A. Yee, "'She Stood in Tears Amid the Alien Corn': Ruth, the Perpetual Foreigner and Model Minority," in *They Were All Together in One Place: Toward Minority Biblical Criticism*, ed. Randall C. Bailey, Tat-Siong Benny Liew, and Fernando F. Segovia (Atlanta: Society of Biblical Literature, 2009), 119–40.

113. Lai Ling Elizabeth Ngan, "Neither Here nor There: Boundary and Identity in the Hagar Story," in *Ways of Being, Ways of Reading: Asian-American Biblical Interpretation*, ed. Mary F. Foskett and Jeffrey K. Kuan (St. Louis: Chalice, 2006), 73 (70–83).

the boundary lines that demarcate her Egyptian identity. Empowered by God who relates to her, addresses her by name, and promises offspring, she audaciously names God and forges a new identity for herself as the mother of a numerous people.[114]

Postcolonial analysis of the Bible emerges particularly with the insertion and challenge of voices from the so-called third world and indigenous peoples into the academic guild, interpreting the Bible from out of their indigenous, postcolonial, or neocolonial contexts. With its shared concerns for the preferential option for the poor, postcolonial biblical criticism is sympathetic to liberation hermeneutics, but proceeds beyond the focus on the economic poor to embrace those marginalized by gender, sexuality, race, ethnicity, culture, colonialism, and religion. Its special focus is on the power relations and disparities between empire and colony, conqueror and conquered, between center and periphery.[115]

One of the most well-known feminist postcolonial biblical scholars is Musa Dube, a black Motswana African, a survivor of colonialism, and in a continual struggle against neocolonialism, where global capitalism is impoverishing most two-thirds world countries with huge debts.[116] In analyzing ancient imperializing texts like the Bible, she asks the following questions:

1. Does this text have a clear stance against the political imperialism of its time?

2. Does this text encourage travel to distant and inhabited lands, and if so, how does it justify itself?

---

114. Ngan explores her Asian American hermeneutics further in Lai Ling Elizabeth Ngan, "Bitter Melon, Bitter Delight: Reading Jeremiah Reading Me," in *Off the Menu: Asian and Asian North American Women's Theology and Religion & Theology*, ed. Rita Nakashima Brock et al. (Louisville: Westminster John Knox, 2007), 163–81; Lai Ling Elizabeth Ngan, "Until Everyone Has a Place under the Sun," in *The Bible and the Hermeneutics of Liberation*, ed. Alejandro F. Botta and Pablo R. Andiñach, Semeia Studies 59 (Atlanta: Society of Biblical Literature, 2009), 213–23.

115. Gale A. Yee, "Postcolonial Biblical Criticism," in *Methods for Exodus*, ed. Thomas B. Dozeman (New York: Cambridge University Press, 2010), 193–233; Bradley L. Crowell, "Postcolonial Studies and the Hebrew Bible," *Currents in Biblical Research* 7, no. 2 (2009): 217–44; Leo G. Perdue and Warren Carter, *Israel and Empire: A Postcolonial History of Israel and Early Judaism* (London: Bloomsbury, 2015).

116. Musa W. Dube, "Toward a Postcolonial Feminist Interpretation of the Bible," *Semeia* 78 (1997): 14.

3. How does this text construct difference: is there dialogue and mutual interdependence, or condemnation and replacement of all that is foreign?

4. Does this text employ gender representations to construct relationships of subordination and domination?[117]

Dube then applies these questions to select passages in the books of Exodus and Joshua to disclose how "the story of Israel's trek from Egypt to the land of Canaan is in every way a God, gold, and glory narrative." It becomes an imperializing story because it is expressly focused on taking and maintaining power over foreign and inhabited lands by divine decree and assistance. The colonizers portray themselves as "chosen," while depicting those they conquer and colonize as deserving invasion, dispossession, subjugation, and annihilation if need be.[118]

In a highly anthologized piece, Cherokee American scholar Laura Donaldson applies postcolonial criticism to the book of Ruth, reading it prismatically through the encounter between Native women and European colonizers. Ruth the Moabite carries the taint of sexuality, because her tribal ancestry can be traced back to the incestuous encounter between Lot and his daughter (Gen 19:36–37) and the Moabite women who seduce Israelite men into idolatry (Num 25:1–3). Thomas Jefferson, the second President of the United States and a framer of its Constitution, compared Ruth's seduction of Boaz to the alleged sexual brazenness of Native women and the sexual impotence of Native men. Facilitating the conquest of indigenous peoples by promoting assimilation, Jefferson encouraged intermarriage between Native women and European men, addressing a delegation of Natives: "in time, you will be as we are; you will become one people with us. Your blood will mix with ours." For Donaldson, the book of Ruth similarly underscores the usefulness of intermarriage in the process of assimilating a non-Jew into the community, where Ruth ultimately disappears.

Both Ruth and her "other" mother-in-law Rahab, the Canaanite prostitute who gives birth to Boaz (Matt 1:5), have analogues with one of Euramerica's signature narratives about Native women, the Pocahontas Perplex. This narrative ideologically constructs Native women as the ones who save or aid white men in their colonization

---

117. Musa Dube, *Postcolonial Feminist Interpretation of the Bible* (St. Louis: Chalice, 2000), 57.
118. Dube, *Postcolonial Feminist Interpretation of the Bible*, 69–70.

of the land. Ruth, in her intermarriage with Boaz, and Rahab, who helps the spies in the conquest of Canaan, represent the stereotype of the indigenous woman who forsakes her native land and aligns herself with the men who will eventually subjugate her and her people. Donaldson does envision a counternarrative in Ruth in the person of Orpah, Ruth's Moabite sister-in-law. Rather than accompanying Naomi and Ruth to Judah, Orpah kisses her mother-in-law goodbye and returns to her mother's house (Ruth 1:8, 14–15). Although Orpah's return has been regarded negatively, "to Cherokee women . . . Orpah connotes hope rather than perversity, because she is the one who does not reject her traditions or her sacred ancestors," but rather chooses "the indigenous mother's house over that of the alien Israelite Father."[119]

Gale A. Yee employs both feminist materialist and postcolonial criticisms in her analysis of Ezekiel 23. Here, the prophet describes the terrible destruction of Jerusalem and the exile of its elites in a passage notable for its pornographic portrait of Israel and Judah as sexually insatiable sisters. Set within the historical context of colonial relations that led to their destruction and exile, she argues that the pornography of the narrative should be coded not simply as another form of patriarchal violence, but as colonial ethnic conflict framed as a sexualized encounter. Similar to constructions of gender in other colonial narratives, Judah and Israel are feminized as the invaded colonized female body, while their foreign conquerors are hypersexualized, with penises "like those of donkeys and whose emission was like that of stallions" (23:20). Ezekiel 23 is the prophet's attempt to deal with the personal and collective trauma of colonization, conquest, and exile of the Judean elite. He absolves his own institutional complicity in the sins of the nation, and that of the male elite class to which he belongs, by projecting the sins of the nation metaphorically onto two sisters, promiscuous from their youth, who suffer sexually violent acts of rape, dismemberment, and destruction.[120]

---

119. Laura E. Donaldson, "The Sign of Orpah: Reading Ruth through Native Eyes," in *Ruth and Esther*, ed. Athalya Brenner, vol. 3, A Feminist Companion to the Bible (Second Series) (Sheffield: Sheffield Academic, 1999), 130–44.

120. Gale A. Yee, "The Two Sisters in Ezekiel: They Played the Whore in Egypt," in *Poor Banished Children of Eve: Woman as Evil in the Hebrew Bible* (Minneapolis: Fortress Press, 2003), 111–34.

CONCLUSION

As we have seen, feminist biblical scholarship rests on a strong foundation of feminist and intersectional scholarship, a scholarship that became conscious of and reacted to its own racism, class bias, colonial privilege, and homophobia over the course of its development. Feminist biblical scholarship began to flourish in the 1960s–1970s, in keeping with the various movements of civil, racial, and gender rights and intellectual unrest occurring during this formative time. In biblical studies, this unrest took shape in the appearance of literary critical studies, reacting to the dominance of historical-critical investigations of the biblical text. Phyllis Trible was the first biblical scholar to apply feminist literary-critical hermeneutics to the Hebrew Bible. Other scholars applied more historical-critical approaches in their own feminist works.

The field of biblical studies itself broadened by adopting interdisciplinary approaches beyond the historical and literary, and feminist biblical scholars were at the forefront of these intellectual inquiries. These scholars embraced insights from postmodern and Marxist/materialist feminists, deconstructionists, queer theorists, and cultural critics to elucidate the Hebrew Bible in invigorating ways. In parallel with these developments, feminist biblicists of color had their own critical interpretations of the text, from their particular situated locations in areas of race, class, colonial or indigenous status, and sexual orientation.

This introduction provides only the tip of the iceberg regarding the current state of feminist and intersectional perspectives on the Hebrew Bible. I hope that it may broaden your own understanding of these issues and help you approach issues of gender, race, and class in the biblical text with greater clarity. In the eager expectation that you will continue to be lifelong learners of the Hebrew Bible, my contributors and I provide examples for further reading at the conclusion of their chapters.

FOR FURTHER READING

Bible and Culture Collective. *The Postmodern Bible*. New Haven: Yale University Press, 1995.

Eskenazi, Tamara Cohn, and Andrea Weiss, eds. *The Torah: A*

Women's Commentary. New York: Women of Reform Judaism, 2008.

Guest, Deryn, Robert E. Goss, Mona West, and Thomas Bohache, eds. *The Queer Bible Commentary.* London: SCM, 2006.

Meyers, Carol, Toni Craven, and Ross S. Kraemer, eds. *Women in Scripture: A Dictionary of Named and Unnamed Women in the Hebrew Bible, the Apocryphal/Deuterocanonical Books, and the New Testament.* Grand Rapids: Eerdmans, 2001.

Newsom, Carol A., Sharon H. Ringe, and Jacqueline E. Lapsley, eds. *Women's Bible Commentary.* 3rd ed., twentieth anniversary ed. Louisville: Westminster John Knox, 2012.

Page, Hugh R., ed. *The Africana Bible: Reading Israel's Scriptures from Africa and the African Diaspora.* Minneapolis: Fortress Press, 2009.

PART I

The Torah/Pentateuch

1.

Character, Conflict, and Covenant in Israel's Origin Traditions

CAROLYN J. SHARP

By means of stories, a community explores how it came into being and what is core to its identity. Storytelling offers defining moments of grace and moments of threat that suggest how to understand the past and the present. Those who preserve their cultural heritage and teach new generations about shared values use stories to sketch charismatic leaders of old, dramatize beginnings and turning points, and render in poignant or inspiring terms what is at stake in the continuing resilience of the community. In order to survive culturally, communities must be malleable and adaptable in the claims they stake.[1] Over time, a community's stories are shaped to assist the process of adaptation: stories are often strategically constructed toward particular aims even when they are grounded in the authentic lived experience of the group. In every community, change is inevitable, because of cultural contact with other groups and also because new perspectives emerge within the community. Storytelling is a foundational way in which a community manages change so that its members can work toward a future in which the community can flourish.

---

1. As Judith Plaskow observes, "Memory is formed and reformed from the interaction of every generation with the fluid richness of Torah. The remembered past provides the basis for a particular present, but the nature of the present also fosters or inhibits particular kinds of memory" (*Standing Again at Sinai: Judaism from a Feminist Perspective* [San Francisco: Harper & Row, 1990], 75).

A community's storytellers are a diverse lot, even in a single period of the community's life. Some may be acknowledged as official guardians of cultural memory: scribes, priests, and those in positions of political power have considerable influence over the ways in which communal history and identity are framed. Other storytellers may enjoy unofficial credentialing: a community may listen to wise elders, those with social power such as patriarchs and matriarchs in extended kinship groups, and those with access to material resources that can benefit the group. Distortion is inevitable in practices of memory, because hierarchies of value organize the ways in which communities think about who they have been and who they are. Not all experiences are deemed worthy of remembering; some memories are considered too dangerous to preserve. Those with less power and those who are actively disenfranchised within a community may find their truths and experiences ignored, downplayed, or relayed in distorted ways. In any community, there are storytellers who feel compelled to speak other truths, who dissent from the official versions of a group's history. The practice of dissent—of challenging official narratives and reframing a community's stories—is vital for the healthy articulation and amplification of a community's self-understanding.

Much of theological value can be gained by feminist inquiry into the sacred texts of ancient Israel. The Torah has been of central importance in rabbinic tradition since before the dawn of the Common Era. The Pentateuch has drawn the attention of Christian interpreters since the earliest days of Christianity; Genesis was regularly the focus of the great preachers of the first centuries, including Origen, Basil the Great, and John Chrysostom. In every age, interpreters work with the Bible according to their cultural norms and the ways in which history, sacred text, and divine revelation are understandable to them. Historical-critical perspectives are essential for our understanding of the Hebrew Scriptures, though historical analysis is only the beginning of understanding biblical books as works of art. Historical analysis guides the reader into a deeper understanding of the theological, social, and political norms and values promoted by different Scripture texts. Every biblical story, poem, and law has been conceived and articulated out of a specific ancient context. Each text was written by a particular author or authors with concrete experiences of social and political empowerment or disenfranchisement, with clarity of vision on certain issues and myopia about others. Each narrative, prophetic oracle, and proverb was written, and many texts later reshaped, toward particular ends that mattered urgently for particular circumstances in which gathered believers needed to be taught about God, their heritage, their religious practices, ethical mandates, leadership, and international politics.

Scribes enjoyed considerable power in the ancient Near East. While some scribes were hired to prepare simple bills of lading and other administrative records, many were by no means simply copyists. Scribes were adept interpreters, public officials, and professional educators who rendered with artfulness and persuasive force the insights of their leaders, priests, prophets, and sages. In any culture, even those in which orality is accorded authority, it is fair to say that with literacy and educational stature comes considerable political power to shape the cultural narratives not only in the present but for generations to come—and in the case of Scripture and other enduring texts, even for millennia. Thus it matters for interpreters interested in cultural performances of power to inquire into the gendered perspectives of ancient scribes.

Female scribes were rare throughout the ancient Near East, though not unknown. It cannot be disputed that the scribes who wrote down and shaped our biblical texts were male and enjoyed elite status as regards education; the same is true for the Babylonian scribes who preserved the *Atrahasis* myth, which has a flood story relevant for interpretation of Genesis; the *Enuma Elish*, which explores motifs of chaos and kingship; and the *Epic of Gilgamesh*, relevant for biblical theological reflections on wisdom and mortality. These sources, along with other traditions and genres from other cultures, doubtless influenced ways in which ancient Israel told its origin stories. In all of these cultures, the valorizing of male authority in credentialed trajectories of public service left little room for the contributions of women. This doesn't mean that the Bible is bereft of stories, songs, prophecies, and aphorisms that may have been uttered by Israelite or Judean women or by those of social classes with less prestige and fewer economic resources. But the governing perspectives and frameworks within which Israel's sacred texts came to be inscribed were thoroughly androcentric and elite. The relative lack of access to professional scribal work also meant less income for ancient women. Restrictions on access to income-producing work has been a means in many times and cultures by which women have been kept from economic security and from accumulating wealth that could be deployed strategically or passed down within families.

Feminist readers may, then, fruitfully inquire into ways in which gender and power are expressed, amplified, distorted, and suppressed in these texts produced by ancient Israel's scribal culture. Gender includes masculinities, too, as a focus of inquiry, as well as a spectrum of femininities and non-normative performances of gender. (Cisgender identity, in which a person's experience of gender aligns well with the gender they were assigned at birth, is just one of many possibilities for gender expression, and there is rich variety within cisgender identity itself.) Female and male bodies, ambiguous or indefinable images of bodiedness, expressions of sexuality, and gendered relationships to power—all of these matter for theology, and all are worthy of feminist examination. This inquiry into the Pentateuch will pursue three goals that lie at the heart of my feminist hermeneutics: to honor all subjects, to interrogate relations of power, and to reform community.[2] First, I claim the conviction that the lived experience of all beings, including nonhuman creatures, should be honored. Feminist biblical criticism seeks to make visible the countless ways in which authoritative sacred texts and their interpretations have lifted up some subjects while marginalizing or suppressing others, and have glorified certain ways of thinking about agency and power while dishonoring and harming subjects who inhabit agency and power in other ways.

Second, I claim the conviction that all relationships involve power (implicit and explicit, unrecognized and overt), and that power should be used with the intention to promote justice, reconciliation, and the flourishing of all beings. Crucial to feminist work is the ongoing interrogation of power relations—to explore how beings and structures are involved with each other, to see what is good and what is harmful, to make known what may be celebrated and what must be resisted.

Third, I claim the conviction that communities always stand in need of reform. Every structured group needs to undergo processes of revision and renewal, dissent and rearticulation, in order to remain responsive to the needs and experiences of its members, to inhabit a just and creative posture toward others, and to work effectively for the flourishing and security—the *shalom*—of all living beings.

2. See Carolyn J. Sharp, "Feminist Queries for Ruth and Joshua: Complex Characterization, Gapping, and the Possibility of Dissent," *SJOT* 28 (2014): 229–52.

The above three trajectories—honoring all subjects, interrogating relations of power, and reforming community—are crucial to feminist work for *shalom* and will be engaged throughout this essay.

Proceeding through Genesis, Exodus, Leviticus, Numbers, and Deuteronomy, we will consider character, conflict, and covenant viewed through a feminist prism. I will lift up for feminist interpretation some aspects of the biblical figures in key stories, with an eye to their moral and political qualities; ways in which dissent, contestation, and violence function in the texts; and the ways in which relational fidelity is framed—both as constraint and as possibility—for the formation and reformation of faithful communities. A theoretically infinite variety of feminist readings could be offered for every text; of necessity, I will focus more substantially on Genesis, Exodus, and Leviticus, with briefer attention to Numbers and Deuteronomy to amplify salient issues. The possibilities articulated here are intended as invitations into the feminist critical landscape. These brief readings and suggestions for theorizing are illustrative, and certainly are not intended as definitive or comprehensive choices.[3] I hope that these considerations of character, conflict, and covenant will help to build the capacity of those who gather around these texts to understand how they may deepen and reconfigure their own subjectivity as faithful readers, interrogate their ways of using and experiencing power toward ever more emancipatory practices, and envision new possibilities for fidelity marked by love of God and love of neighbor.

Before turning to the five books of the Pentateuch, I offer a word about the character of the God who acts and speaks throughout Israel's sacred narratives. Particular emphases and points of divine characterization have long been distinguished among the various sources (priestly, nonpriestly, and Deuteronomic[4]). But because Israel's ancient traditions have been deftly interwoven, the reader

---

3. An excellent starting place for feminist theorizing of Hebrew Bible scholarship is the work of Esther Fuchs. See her "Reclaiming the Hebrew Bible for Women: The Neoliberal Turn in Contemporary Feminist Scholarship," *JFSR* 24 (2008): 45–65; "Biblical Feminisms: Knowledge, Theory and Politics in the Study of Women in the Hebrew Bible," *BibInt* 16 (2008): 205–26.

4. Distinctions are evident among the Pentateuchal sources' treatments of women. Sarah Shectman offers, "Women in P's [priestly] narratives appear almost entirely in relation to men. . . . The culmination of the trend to subsume women to men . . . comes in P's hallmark text, the promise and covenant with Abraham in Genesis 17. . . . The relatively diverse women's traditions preserved in non-P disappear almost entirely in P" (*Women in the Pentateuch: A Feminist and Source-Critical Analysis*, HBM 23 [Sheffield: Sheffield Phoenix, 2009], 178).

encounters God in the Pentateuch as a complex single agent. Consequently, the below discussion will not privilege source-critical distinctions but will treat each biblical book as an artful whole.

DIVINE CHARACTER IN THE PENTATEUCH

The most powerful agent in the biblical narratives is God. The Creator speaks the cosmos into existence, constrains human violence and directs the burgeoning of human political culture, and guides untested leaders into the accomplishment of extravagant divine promises. Working miraculous acts of deliverance at every turn, the Lord sustains the Israelites as they move through a threatening wilderness landscape on the journey toward Canaan. God as Lawgiver gives Israel the gift of norms and practices that form Israel as a holy people ethically grounded in love of neighbor and care for the widow, orphan, and resident alien. In all of these texts, through the beautiful variety of dictions and diverse traditions, God is consistently voiced and imagined as an all-powerful male. God's metaphorical maleness, reinforced innumerable times within the Torah at the level of plot and also grammatically via masculine verbs and pronouns, presents profound challenges for feminist theology. Imagining a deity as male was not the only option for theological thinking in the ancient Near East, nor was it a "natural" choice in the millennia that followed in the many cultures that have cherished Israel's sacred texts. Portraying God as male is a product of tenacious patriarchal distortions that privilege male bodiedness and roles that have been accorded disproportionately to males (king, warrior, priest, sage) in their ideologies of divinity.

The feminist interpreter may work with a number of significant moments in the characterization of God. The spirit/wind hovering over the face of the deep at the dawn of creation (Gen 1:2) is grammatically feminine; while grammatical gender has no necessary connection to gendered subjectivity, creative feminist readings have claimed a brooding maternal presence at the beginning of God's action bringing order out of primordial chaos. The plurality inscribed within the divine likeness in Genesis 1:26–27 ("let us make humankind in our image, according to our likeness . . . male and female") has suggested to feminist interpreters a spectrum of gender possibilities honored in the divine Person. The mystery of YHWH's self-identification to Moses at the burning bush ("I am who I am" or "I will be who I will be," Exod 3:14) might serve as a resource for feminist interpretations that position God and God's people at the edges of conventional systematic theology. In the Holiness Code, the Lord's command that Israel "be holy, for I the Lord your God am holy" (Lev 19:2) may be claimed as a feminist warrant to resist and reform whatever in human culture distorts or undermines the holy truth of believers, including the lived experience of women, queer folks, and others who have been kept on the margins of institutional religion. The mobility of the tabernacle (see e.g. Num 9:15–23) may be refracted through a feminist lens to envision the sustaining presence of God in every new terrain—spiritual, political, social—into which God's people journey. Finally, powerful for feminist hermeneutics is the core theological claim of ancient Israel that God is one who can "perform marvels, such as have not been performed in all the earth or in any nation" (Exod 34:10). This earth has not yet seen thoroughgoing justice for women and girls, or for men who perform masculinity in non-normative ways, or for other gender and sexual minorities, or for other constituents disprivileged in countless intersectional ways by misogyny, racism, homophobia, transphobia, poverty, and other systemic affronts to human flourishing. When feminists read ancient narratives and poems lauding God as incomparable wonder-worker, we may dare to hope that radical transformation toward justice may yet be possible for those who suffer under the explicit violence and subtle brutalities of patriarchy.

GENESIS

The book of Genesis tells of the creating of the universe and the calling of the original ancestor, Abram, whose lineage would become God's covenant people Israel. The two creation accounts bring into dialogical relationship two different ways of thinking theologically. A priestly voice, which scholars trace to ancient scribes associated with the Jerusalem Temple, eloquently hymns the beauty of divinely structured order (1:1—2:4a); then comes a nonpriestly voice that speaks in a register of ambiguity and tension as the story unfolds with the Lord God and humankind (2:4b—3:24). The feminist interpreter may hear in the interplay of these ancient sources the possibility—present from the dawn of sacred storytelling, as it were—for multiple voices to speak their truths in community: here is feminist warrant for the position that no voice need yield to another's official narrative. Yet the divine speech that positions humankind at the apex of the creational hierarchy ("let them have dominion over the fish of the sea, and over the birds of the air, and over the cattle, and over the wild animals of the earth, and over every creeping thing," 1:26) presents a challenge for feminist visions of mutuality within the bioecology of all living creatures. The story of Adam and Eve offers many angles of fascination for the feminist reader regarding the power to name, the nature of sexed and gendered relationship, and the consequences of choosing wisdom over obedience to received norms. The flood story illustrates the gravity of the ways in which humans harm one another: the destruction of almost all living things was caused by humanity's tendency toward evil. Narratives about the patriarchs and matriarchs of Israel explore tensions between those who are privileged and those who look on from the margins. The Joseph cycle offers the feminist reader much to mull regarding insider and outsider status, the risks of assimilation, and the ways in which the personal and the political are interwoven.

The presence of some strong female characters notwithstanding, Genesis enshrines the power of heterosexual males. Those are the agents whose actions shape the course of Israel's history. Female subjectivity is not a focus, nor are queer or other performances of sexual or gender identity accounted for. The genealogies and ethnographies in Genesis 4, 5, 10, 11, and 36 are patrilineal; names of women who carried, gave birth to, and nursed the children are almost never recorded. A stark illustration of this can be found in Genesis 4. There, the three sons of Lamech are described as "the ancestor of those who live in tents and have livestock," "the ancestor of all who play the lyre and pipe," and one "who made all kinds of bronze and iron tools"; of the female child, the text offers only, "the sister of Tubal-cain was Naamah" (4:20–22). Throughout the Pentateuch, attention to the male and subordination of the female are presented narratologically as natural and not worthy of comment.

The garden of Eden story offers fertile soil for feminist analysis. The priority of the man (being created first; having the power to name the animals and the woman) has been taken as authoritative grounds for male gender privilege for centuries. The active role of the woman in the episode with the serpent has been mustered to support negative, even viciously misogynist understandings of women's spiritual and moral capacities from the beginning of the Common Era to the present day. Feminist readers have resisted the perceived gender hierarchy in these texts. Phyllis Trible argued on the basis of Hebrew narratological and grammatical features that the first human was a sexually undifferentiated "earth creature" that became male and female only upon the Lord God's creation of the woman.[5] Feminist readers have lauded Eve's initiative in seeking wisdom. Some suggest that the divinely ordained consequences for disobedience detailed in Genesis 3—increased pain in childbearing and the experience of male dominion for the woman; unremitting toil for the man—should be understood as explanations of flawed reality rather than prescriptions for how gender roles should be. Interpreters considering the arc of Genesis 1–3 have argued that the expulsion of the humans from the garden was necessary for the ancestors to fulfill the divine command to "be fruitful and multiply, and fill the earth" (1:28). Such readings of the garden story affirm Eve's desire for wisdom as discernment that makes possible the fulfilling of God's first command.

Three traditions of the patriarchs jeopardizing the well-being of their wives provide case studies in the complexities of character in Genesis. In Genesis 12, Abram preemptively lies about his wife, handing Sarai over to sexual service of the Egyptian pharaoh out of anxiety for his own safety. The Lord punishes the Egyptian royal court with plagues until Abram and Sarai depart; through this development, the biblical narrator suggests the appalling nature of Abram's choice to compromise Sarai's body but, as often occurs in ancient Hebrew narrative, does not indicate disapproval of the moral failing of the patriarch. The reader is left to draw what was surely a transparently obvious conclusion. In Genesis 20, Abraham perpetrates the same ruse; Abimelech of Gerar takes Sarah into his harem but has not yet violated her when he is warned by God in a dream. The chastened king appeases Abraham with livestock, slaves, and a thousand pieces of silver (20:14, 16), the narrator showing the potential gravity of the near-offense by highlighting the extravagant nature of the gifts. An ancient Israelite hearer, steeped in cultural norms that required males to guard the sexual purity of female kin, would have been shocked at Abra(ha)m. Feminist interpretation will name Abraham's betrayal of his spouse as a hallmark of patriarchy's continual commodification of women's bodies for sexual slavery, political security, and economic gain. In Genesis 26, a third reflex of

---

5. Phyllis Trible, *God and the Rhetoric of Sexuality*, OBT (Philadelphia: Fortress Press, 1978), 72–143.

this tradition takes care to show that the matriarch is never violated: Isaac puts his wife Rebecca in jeopardy, but the king of Gerar is shown to be hyperscrupulous in foreclosing potential avenues of harm to her. The flawed character of the two patriarchs, and especially Abram, is on view in these risks to God's covenant promise of offspring. Anxiety about risk to the masculine subject is pervasive in patriarchal cultures, because violence is inherent in phallocentrism, the ideology that the needs of the phallus, understood in literal and metaphorical terms, should govern social and political relations. In these stories of a patriarch jeopardizing the well-being of his wife, we glimpse an age-old battle for power that inevitably involves collateral damage to female bodies.

Hagar has long fascinated feminist interpreters, who celebrate her resilience in the face of the Egyptian slave's economic and sexual subordination within the household of Abraham and Sarah.[6] The stories of the banishment of Hagar highlight the competition for social status between Sarah and Hagar, something true to the experiences of many women in polygynous tribal cultures and other systemic reflexes of patriarchy. Responding to angelic deliverance in the desert, Hagar dares to name God ("You are El-roi," 16:13; perhaps "God who sees," suggesting that the Lord has taken account of the subjection of this desperate outcast and her child). This subversive moment in ancient Hebrew literature has proved a powerful resource for feminist solidarity with the marginalized.

The story of Abraham's near-sacrifice of Isaac (Gen 22:1–19) has been taken as a paradigm for faith that privileges obedience to divine command over the sanctity of life and familial bonds of love and trust. Interpreters have wrestled for millennia with the horrifying nature of the premise (22:12, 15–18) that unquestioning obedience within a regime of hierarchical power can justify an atrocity and be rewarded with blessing. Feminist interpreters do not valorize naïve obedience in distorted power relations here; they decline to concede the authorization of the Holy behind such cultural norms. Genesis 22 and its reception history constitute a standing invitation to feminist readers to rework ancient notions of divine power, proffering new visions of the sacred that do not rely on the brutal slaughter of innocents.

Conflict pervades the book of Genesis. These narratives brim with

---

6. See the iconic treatment of Hagar in Delores S. Williams, *Sisters in the Wilderness: The Challenge of Womanist God-Talk*, 20th anniversary ed. (Maryknoll, NY: Orbis, 2013).

violence, in overt forms in which persons are beaten, raped, or killed and in subtler forms in which individuals and families suffer devastating moral injury or psychological harm. Cain's murder of his brother Abel (Genesis 4) portrays fratricide within the matrix of agonistic politics concerning sacrifice. The vivid image of the blood of Abel crying out from the ground (4:10) renders in unforgettable terms the pathos of homicide. Feminists may draw upon that image to raise awareness about the terrible injustices suffered by women, children, non-normative men, and folks of other genders under the brutalities of phallocratic hierarchy. God punishing Cain with perpetual wandering while also protecting Cain from being killed invites feminist analysis of ways in which the authorization of privilege continues even for perpetrators of extreme harm.

Conflict in familial relationships is explored in three other trajectories in Genesis: the cycle of stories about Jacob and Esau, the narratives about Leah and Rachel, and the material about Joseph and his brothers. Trickster Jacob manipulates his father Isaac and brother Esau until Esau simmers with homicidal rage (Gen 27:41) and Jacob must flee. On the eve of reunion with Esau, Jacob is attacked by a divine emissary (32:22–32), the struggle seen by some interpreters as symbolic of the turmoil within Jacob's psyche or as a spiritual dramatization of the conflict within the kinship group. The narrative of reconciliation between Jacob and Esau (33:1–17), fraught though it is with tension as the brothers strive for control, might be explored by feminists as an illustration of antagonists moving beyond old scripts into a more equitable relationship. No such reconciliation is obtained in the bitter enmity between sisters Leah and Rachel as they compete for social power via the birth of sons (Genesis 29–30). Feminist interpreters have observed the deleterious effects of cultural norms that constrain women's pathways to social power. When public leadership, artistic and educational positions, priestly or other liturgical roles, and similar avenues are forbidden to women, they may perceive that sexuality and childbearing are their chief means of economic security and advancement in status. The privileging of sons for inheritance rights was a central feature of ancient Israelite social polity, so much was at stake for entire clans in the birth of sons; infertility was experienced as socially shaming and could constitute an economic disaster. Economic inequities based on gender do many kinds of damage to the subjectivity of women and girls; the damage extends also to males and others whose roles are scripted by systems that harm their family members and neighbors.

Conflict in the cycle of Joseph stories (Genesis 37–50) is relevant for feminist interpretation not least because of the dynamics of investiture and subjugation that operate through the story, and because of the hybridity of Joseph's identity as Israelite and Egyptian. This artful narrative illumines ways in which privilege can generate responses of hostility, while ingenuity in circumstances of powerlessness can lead to renewed social capital and political authority. Joseph's reinvention of himself as an influential Egyptian may be analyzed in a number of productive ways, including as a powerful claim for reconfiguration of identity under duress and as a queering of normative strictures on cultural mixing. That is, the culturally strict separation between "Israelite" and "Other" visible in many ancient Israelite traditions is here resisted and revised: in a single story and a single body, Joseph is both Israelite hero and Egyptian overlord.

Sexual violence against females and nondominant males is a pervasive feature of patriarchal cultures. The story of the Lord's obliteration of Sodom (Genesis 18–19) has generated much homophobic interpretation, as if the absurdly hyperbolic sexual violence threatened by the denizens of that city may fairly be predicated of others oriented toward same-sex relations. The callousness with which Lot offers his daughters for gang-rape may have been intended to illustrate a pervasive flaw in the character of the men in Terah's line, since Abraham's and Isaac's failure to protect their wives from sexual commodification may be framed in similar terms.[7] This story highlights how little the well-being of females matters within a phallocentric social framework: the narrative focuses entirely on Lot, the visiting angels, and the men of Sodom, and no voice or perspective is accorded Lot's daughters, something also true in the story of the gang-rape, death, and dismemberment of the Levite's concubine in Judges 19. The story of the rape of Dinah (Genesis 34) illustrates how much can be at stake for ethnic groups in situations of economic or political precarity. Men granting sexual access to their group's women through marriage conceived as a transitive transaction can function as a form of trade or political

7. See Susanne Scholz, "Rape, Enslavement, and Marriage: Sexual Violence in the Hebrew Bible," in *Introducing the Women's Hebrew Bible*, Introductions in Feminist Theology 13 (New York: T&T Clark, 2007), 76–99.

treaty. In patriarchal cultures such as ancient Israel, where family status is influenced by metrics of honor and shame calibrated in relation to phallocentric social norms, the sexual purity of women is guarded by male kin as a matter of honor. That female bodies are regularly violated, then commodified in extrajudicial responses such as vigilante vengeance, shows how robustly phallocentrism suffuses the ideology of these social groups. Feminists have highlighted as significant that Dinah is silenced within the narrative and have critiqued readings in the history of reception that perpetuate harmful ideologies regarding males' accountability for sexual violence and ways in which female social initiative may be misunderstood as inviting assault. Masculine hypocrisy has drawn the attention of feminist interpreters also in Genesis 38, a nuanced story where the widowed Tamar tricks her father-in-law into impregnating her, then escapes immolation because she is able to expose his accountability.

At the cessation of the flood (Gen 9:1–17), God promises to honor every living creature and forswears any future violence at a world-destroying level. Feminist advocacy for social and ecological justice could draw on this covenantal promise when elaborating on ways in which the well-being of the powerless might be secured through new practices of *shalom*. God's promises of land and progeny to Abraham, articulated in 12:1–3 and other iterations, provide much grist for feminist reflection. Where "fear and dread" of humans were to be the enduring portion of nonhuman creatures under the Noahide covenant (9:2), something that bespoke a model of domination problematic for feminist interpretation, "all the families of the earth" are to know abundant blessing through Abram (12:3), suggesting mutual accountability and respect. Yet the Abrahamic covenant also provides authorization for Israel's invasion and plunder of inhabited territories and slaughter of indigenous peoples. The God of the patriarchs is understood in Israel's sacred traditions to require that Israel dispossess, enslave, and exterminate Canaanite groups ("the Kenites, the Kenizzites, the Kadmonites, the Hittites, the Perizzites, the Rephaim, the Amorites, the Canaanites, the Girgashites, and the Jebusites," 15:19–21) in order to come into the "inheritance" that God has promised. Militarized invasion and cultural imperialism are inextricable from the covenantal traditions in Genesis, a matter of grave concern to feminist interpreters.

Finally, it may be observed that circumcision as an indelible marker of covenantal identity is first commanded in Genesis (17:9–14; see also Lev 12:3). Clearly the unassailable preeminence of the male subject is foregrounded here. There is no parallel ritual or inscribed marker of identity for females within the Israelite community, and males with damaged genitals are expressly barred from belonging to the covenant community (Deut 23:1). The non-negotiable centrality of the actual phallus in the religious ideology of Israel's covenantal traditions has yielded many kinds of repercussions and consequences critiqued by feminists.

EXODUS

Throughout the centuries, many readers have found inspirational the story of God's deliverance of Israel from slavery in Egypt. The Exodus tradition has been used by feminist and other liberation theologians to ground the claim that God is on the side of the marginalized, hears the cries of the oppressed (see Exod 2:23–25; 3:7–10), and intervenes in human history to unseat the mighty and lift up the poor. Black theologians, Marxist readers, queer commentators, and others committed to hermeneutics of emancipation have mined the Exodus story to articulate their hopes for political justice for the enslaved and those dehumanized by racism, economic justice for the poor, justice for gender and sexual minorities, and the increase of *shalom* generally in a world riven by inequity and brutality. The events of the exodus are sparked by Egyptian exploitation and repression of the burgeoning Israelite community as a reflex of fear of the Other (1:7–14). Feminists theorize such subjugation within a larger intersectional framework in which patriarchal power has been valorized as domination in many ways within different but related arenas of life in community. When the Egyptians assert power by seeking to suppress the enslaved Israelites' population, the Hebrew midwives Shiphrah and Puah emerge as models of courage and ingenuity. Declining to collaborate with the Egyptian order to slaughter Israelite male newborns, the midwives are rewarded in the biblical plot and lauded in interpretive tradition thereafter. Shiphrah and Puah offer us a glimpse of the agency of ancient women who worked effectively on behalf of their communities in roles that were vital to the well-being of families and communities.

The contest of wonders and plagues that unfolds between Moses and the Egyptian pharaoh (Exodus 5–12) is theologized as a means by which God displays divine power in the sight of the Egyptians and other nations (see e.g. 7:5; 9:16; 10:1–2; 14:18; 18:10–11). The Exodus tradition was forged, narratively speaking, in irresolvable conflict. The conflict between the Lord and the Egyptian pharaoh proceeds along a trajectory that is not typical of struggles for domination within human culture. It begins as a contest to showcase each ruler's authority over the forces of the natural world, though of course in the perspective of the ancient writers, the Lord as Creator of the cosmos wields authentic power over water, creatures, and sky; Pharaoh's magicians can only mimic some of the effects achieved by the deity. The Egyptian opponent is being controlled by the Lord, who has made Pharaoh obstinate so that he will not release Israel and the contest for glory can continue. The Lord says to Pharaoh, "By now I could have stretched out my hand and struck you and your people with pestilence, and you would have been cut off from the earth, but this is why I have let you live: to show you my power, and to make my name resound through all the earth" (9:15–16), and to Moses, "I have hardened his [Pharaoh's] heart and the heart of his officials, in order that I may show these signs of mine among them, and that you may tell your children and grandchildren how I have made fools of the Egyptians" (Exod 10:1–2). A variety of feminist analyses are possible here, as with any biblical text or tradition. Some feminist interpreters might celebrate the matchless power of God to shame oppressive human rulers for the cause of justice. Other feminists might critique this discourse as a predictable reflex of patriarchal masculinity. The death of Egyptian noncombatants and children in the final plague troubles even feminists who affirm the necessity of violence as an integral part of resistance to domination. The lives of Egyptian women, children, and noncombatant males are worthless in this battle between the Lord and the pharaoh, and one might observe that the Israelites remain enslaved for longer than necessary, to bolster the glorification of masculine divine power. For many feminists, a more authentic vision of the Holy will need to reframe the struggles for supremacy that were so essential to the ancient Near Eastern imagination. Nevertheless, the appeal of the Exodus tradition as liberatory has been strong and enduring.

Equally catalytic for feminist visions of emancipation is the long arc of the exodus after the Israelites' liberation from slavery. The Israelites persevere, with divine accompaniment and wise leadership from Moses, in a forty-year journey through wilderness terrain toward freedom. To be sure, some feminists balk at calling "freedom," as liberation theologians do, a militarized invasion of Canaan and extermination of its inhabitants. But Israel's wilderness wandering has been claimed by many as a model of hope during their own debilitating struggles for social change. On the way to Canaan, Israel faces crippling fear of the unknown, lack of clean water, dearth of food, battle with indigenous groups, internecine revolt, and the deadly havoc wreaked repeatedly by a God who waxes wrathful at signs of disobedience. That Israel survives these risks and harms may be interpreted by feminists as relevant to their own resistance in the face of the deprivations, assaults, and micro-aggressions of patriarchal social and political systems.

Writ larger than life is the spectacular character of Moses. The commissioning of Moses offers a marvelous paradigm for the gradual growth of feminist awareness, political conscientization, and emerging leadership. Vulnerable as a baby afloat in a papyrus basket, then rescued and reared in potentially hostile surroundings (Exodus 2), Moses comes to understand his true identity only when the divine Voice calls from the burning bush to lay out the vocation that has been prepared for him (Exodus 3). Incipient leaders who would embrace a feminist vision can be daunted by the precarious political circumstances in which they may find themselves. The story of Moses may be claimed by feminists as a sign of hope for their own survival in an alien land, resilience in the face of obstacles and threats, and eventual leadership of other constituents desperate for freedom. Of course, Moses's character as leader may also be interpreted as problematic by feminists committed to nonviolent transformation. Responding to the beating of an Israelite by an Egyptian, Moses murders the Egyptian man, hides the corpse, and flees, a sequence of events that has troubled many interpreters over the centuries. Later, one of the most chilling commands in all of Scripture comes from the mouth of Moses when he witnesses uncontrolled malfeasance in the Israelite camp after the debacle of the Golden Calf. Claiming to speak for the Lord, Moses thunders, "Put your sword on your side, each of you [Levites]! Go back and forth from gate to gate throughout the camp, and each of you kill your brother, your friend, and your neighbor" (Exod 32:27). As with Abraham before him, and as will be the case with King David later in Israel's history, so the character of Moses is drawn with attention to dimensions of malfeasance that have given pause to readers since ancient times. One salutary lesson for the feminist reader may be this: idolizing any biblical character as worthy of uncritical emulation is something that the biblical narrative seeks to deflect. That said, it may be noted that the character of Miriam has long sparked the feminist imagination. Identified as a prophet and described as leading liturgical celebration after Israel has crossed the Red Sea (Exod 15:20–21), Miriam also dares to stand up to Moses and claim her own authority (Num 12:1–2). While few details are offered in the relevant ancient narratives, the feminist interpreter may reconstruct a powerful leader in Miriam, traces of whose agency could not be erased even by the thoroughgoing androcentrism of Israel's scribal tradition.

Dramatic conflict at the foot of Sinai invites feminist reflection on communal misperceptions of the divine and on ideology veiled in storytelling. The Golden Calf episode (Exodus 32) is narrated artfully to illustrate the lure of syncretism, the risk of misguided faith in that which cannot save, and the importance of obliterating dissent. Whether the golden statue is meant to be seen as representing YHWH in an illegitimate way or as drawing on tauromorphic (bull-shaped) imagery from Egyptian or another religion to create an outright idol, it is understood as an affront that merits extreme punishment: the Levites make free to slaughter other Israelites, and a divinely ordained plague is unleashed (32:25–35). The story's interest in underlining the culpability of Aaron may point to internecine disputes within priestly circles in the Second Temple period (from 538 BCE until the Jerusalem Temple was destroyed in 70 CE). If the point had been to disenfranchise Aaronide priests politically, that would be a subterranean ideological aim that is not evident on the surface of the Golden Calf story. The feminist remembers, when interpreting this and all biblical texts, that the ideological purposes for which authoritative texts are composed and shaped may be quite different from what the stories seem to be about. Over against the purist zealotry that triumphs in the Golden Calf story, feminists might reframe syncretism as a fruitful means by which believers in many times and places have sought to understand the sacred truths of others, honoring what they can without compromising their own convictions. What cannot save, for many who have been disastrously harmed or marginalized in heteropatriarchy and extremist religions, is distorted theologizing about a deity who doesn't hesitate to kill those out of step with doctrinal orthodoxy. Dissent, for feminist interpreters, is a vital tool for reformation of power structures that subjugate and destroy.[8] A feminist interpreter might bring into fruitful dialogue the Golden Calf story and an ancient theological refrain proclaimed by God shortly afterwards: "The Lord, the Lord, a God merciful and gracious, slow to anger, and abounding in steadfast love and faithfulness, keeping steadfast love for the thousandth generation, forgiving iniquity and transgression and sin" (34:6–7). The refrain occurs several times in the Hebrew Scriptures (see Num 14:18; Deut 7:9–10; Neh 9:17; Pss 86:15; 103:8; 145:8), sometimes, as here in Exodus, amplified by a comment about God punishing the guilty. The claim invited ongoing theological reflection within Scripture, as we can see from its deployment in the Book of the Twelve (see Joel 2:13; Jonah 4:2; and Nah 1:3).

God's covenant with Israel is narrated in Exodus through three modes of discourse that invite feminist analysis: the portrayal of God as Divine Warrior (Exodus 14–15), the story of God's giving of the Law on Sinai (Exodus 20–23), and the attention lavished on details of the Tabernacle with its furnishings and personnel (Exodus 25–31, 35–40). Israel's origin stories, Law and ritual practices, prophetic literature, and liturgical poetry all draw on recitals of God's military deliverance of Israel. The power of this liberatory tradition is such that even pacifists have found their spirits stirred by the image of God as Warrior marching forth on behalf of the oppressed. The God who is faithful to Israel in covenantal relationship is a God who redeems the covenant people with a mighty hand (Exod 13:9), a military metonym. As Moses reassures the Israelites, "The Lord will fight for you, and you have only to keep still" (14:14). God as Divine Warrior is hymned in the songs of Moses and Miriam (Exodus 15), and the martial personification of God is utilized in the book of Joshua, Psalm 68, Isaiah 63, and many other Hebrew Bible texts. Whether and how to draw on this metaphor, constructed as it is on the life-crushing practices of actual human warfare, is a question that each feminist interpreter needs to consider. Those who subscribe to a form of just war theory and those who claim the appropriateness of strategic violence as a tool of political resistance will be more comfortable with the ancient tradition of God as Warrior than those who insist that

---

8. On dissent as crucial in feminist work, see Ewa Płonowska Ziarek, *An Ethics of Dissensus: Postmodernity, Feminism, and the Politics of Radical Democracy* (Stanford: Stanford University Press, 2003).

violence runs counter to the ethical mandates of love and justice on which authentic feminism is built.

God's giving of the Law is of key importance for feminist interpretation. The regulation of life in community is crucially important for collaborative articulation of shared norms, protection of the weak, restitution of loss, and reform of harmful practices. Yet the enforcing of statutes has also been used since the dawn of jurisprudence to restrict and punish individuals and groups in unjust and lethal ways. Some aspects of case law will be discussed in the treatment of Leviticus below. Here in Exodus, we may consider the connection of theology with the shaping of communal history. The Ten Commandments (20:1–17) tie Israel's obligations for right worship, observance of the Sabbath, and ethical behavior to the identity of God as the one "who brought you out of the land of Egypt, out of the house of slavery" (Exod 20:1). Divine deliverance requires reciprocal obedience, expressed as reverence for God and the honoring of others in the covenant community. Feminists may take this foundational calculus and extend it in robust and compelling ways. Make no idol? Then feminists must dismantle all of the ways in which cisgender, heteronormative, white supremacist, and economically unjust models have been set up as cultural norms worthy of adulation. Make no wrongful use of the name of the Lord? Then feminists are bound to resist all the ways in which religious orthodoxy has been used to subjugate and suppress the embodied flourishing of others made in the image of God. Do not kill? Though ancient Israel did not intend for capital punishment to be included under this statute, the contemporary feminist hermeneut should work passionately for the reform of unjust carceral practices, including state-sponsored execution, that crush the spirits and destroy the lives of so many. Do not covet? Then feminist cultural critics must work tirelessly to resist the engines of economic greed and the fetishizing of materialism that drive global capitalism.

Finally, Exodus offers as a mode of covenantal fidelity a long narrative that delights in the details of construction, furnishing, and staffing of the Tabernacle. Precious materials are dedicated and artisanally deployed to create an exquisite holy space for the God who accompanies Israel on their journey. Faithfulness here is expressed through descriptions of vessels of gold, silver, and bronze, lustrous acacia wood with gold or bronze overlay, cups shaped like almond blossoms with delicately wrought calyxes and petals, curtains of fine linen with blue, purple, and crimson embroidery, and magnificent priestly vestments skillfully made with fine textiles, gems, and gold filigree. Feminist interpreters may be energized as we consider the breathtaking beauty of holiness and the preciousness of life lived in fidelity. Feminists can beckon others into creativity—through art, music, film, storytelling, dance, and other paths—as witness to the ways in which we honor God, celebrate the image of the Holy in one another, and transform our communities.

LEVITICUS

In this complex book, the feminist reader encounters ancient laws and statutes intended to govern Israel's organization as a holy people. The official norms of a body politic can serve effectively to safeguard the weak and marginalized and to build the capacity of a community to respond in equitable ways to economic disputes and injury, but laws can also be used to support and maintain the political power of the ruling class or elite individuals over against the rights and flourishing of others. Leviticus inscribes regulatory gestures in a detailed and multilayered corpus of possibilities, some of which are unquestionably harmful to the well-being of members of the community imagined in that biblical book, and some of which are beneficial.

Within the ancient Israelite sacrificial system, male priests ritually slaughtered healthy livestock and birds, not only for provision of food—though priests and others were indeed sustained by consuming parts of the offerings—but as a means of rendering a creature's life as an offering to God on behalf of the covenant community so that God could continue to reside with the people. Male animals were privileged for the burnt offering and purification offering (Lev 1:3, 10; 4:3, 14, 23), except in cases regarding an unintentional sin committed by an ordinary person rather than by a priest, the whole community, or a ruler (4:28). Pragmatically, the keeping of breeding-age female animals from the ritual knife would have ensured the continual production of new offspring. But the feminist interpreter might also consider a cultural ethos that privileges the male in many dimensions of public life to be operative in this hierarchy. Compassion for the economically disprivileged is expressed in the sacrificial system through permitting those with reduced material resources to bring less costly animals to sacrifice (e.g., 5:7, 11; 12:8;

14:21), and also through the release of indentured servants and return of arable land to its original owners in the Year of Jubilee (25:10–17), though the latter practice could also serve to reinforce elite families' control of wealth. The sacrificial system is designed to honor the holiness of God through a detailed set of interventions that maintain or repair the covenant relationship between deity and people. The cultural logic is articulated as "keep[ing] the people of Israel separate from their uncleanness, so that they do not die in their uncleanness by defiling my tabernacle that is in their midst" (15:31; see also 20:22–26). Illegitimate ritual offenses can be punishable by immediate divine execution, as in the case of Nadab and Abihu (10:1–3; compare the fate of Uzzah in 2 Samuel 6–7). Nothing less than the glory of God is considered to be at stake in Israel's appropriate observance of ritual practices. Separation from other peoples and abstention from their ritual practices—named as abhorrent by ancient Israelite scribes—are vital for the ongoing life of Israel as a people dedicated to the worship of YHWH. The Lord makes this clear over and over: "You shall not do as they do in the land of Egypt, where you lived, and you shall not do as they do in the land of Canaan. . . . You shall keep my statutes and my ordinances; by doing so one shall live; I am the Lord" (18:3, 5).

Feminist interpreters of all genders find it important to analyze the statutes regulating female and male bodies. Ritual impurity should not be confused with moral impurity, even though ritual uncleanness does affect that which it touches and thus must be contained. For a body to require ritual time apart or ritual cleansing is not pejorative or demeaning in any moral sense. Yet feminists may spy signals of phallocentrism and stigmatizing of the female in the system, for example in the statute requiring a longer period of purification after a woman gives birth to a female child than for a male child (12:1–5), in the requirement that a priest marry only a woman who is a virgin (20:13–14), and in legislation that suggests that female sex workers are in a state of permanent defilement (21:7, 14). LGBTQ readers and their allies will need to analyze with a robust hermeneutics of suspicion the legislation prohibiting male same-sex relations as an "abomination" (18:22; 20:13). Every feminist interpreter will find repellent the statute allowing Israelites to take male and female slaves "from the nations around you" and hold them as property for generations (25:44–46). For some feminists, the virulent homophobic ideology, privileging of cisgender heteronormativity more generally, and disgracefully permissive approach to slaveholding that we read in Leviticus may render suspect even the more benign aspects of ancient Israelite case law. Feminists rightly celebrate the statutes that require compassion be shown the poor and the resident alien (19:9–10, 33–34), even as they critique the prejudicial logic underlying restrictive regulation of those within the priesthood who experience temporary or permanent disability (21:16–23). A host of feminist practices of restorative justice may be funded by observance of the injunction to "love your neighbor as yourself" (19:18; compare also 19:34), a commandment that has enjoyed a rich history of interpretation in the New Testament (Matt 22:34–40; Mark 12:28–34; Luke 10:25–37) and beyond.

Feminist interpreters may note that the book of Leviticus constructs several different implied subjects through its halakhic discourse. The first subject is God. The Lord speaks the words of Leviticus and is the voice of authority—no dissent is brooked, and no dialogue is invited. This leaves the deity, as agent in Leviticus, with unassailable power to direct the behavior of individual Israelites and their community in a way that is not analogous in nonpriestly material in Genesis, where Abraham bargains with the deity (Genesis 18), or in Exodus, where Moses successfully intercedes and changes the trajectory of divine action (Exod 32:7–14). The God portrayed in Leviticus is mighty to save and to protect, but God will not hesitate to punish mercilessly when the people go astray. Leviticus 26 dwells with relish on a series of horrifying consequences that God threatens to level against the covenant people if they disobey: "I will bring terror on you; consumption and fever that waste the eyes and cause life to pine away. . . . I will let loose wild animals against you, and they shall bereave you of your children. . . . You shall eat the flesh of your sons, and you shall eat the flesh of your daughters. . . . I will heap your carcasses on the carcasses of your idols. . . . As for those of you who survive, I will send faintness into their hearts in the lands of their enemies; the sound of a driven leaf shall put them to flight" (see the entire catalog of punishments, 26:14–39; similarly gruesome curses are on view in Deuteronomy 28). Readers of Leviticus are to imagine as subjects the obedient believer and the miscreant, writ collectively as a plural "you" who might follow God's commandments and observe them faithfully or might be hostile to God and not obey. Feminist interpretation may inquire into how the fate of the community is inscribed in a collective subject in this way, such that the less powerful in the community—those who have no access to positions of public decision-making—must yoke their fates to the choices made by those in power. On ethical grounds, feminists committed to honoring all subjects, interrogating relations of power, and reforming community may find the implied theology here to be execrable.

Regularly in Leviticus, we are invited to imagine a male subject as the norm. While many of the statutes regarding moral and ethical behavior apply to all in the covenant community, it is also the case that requirements for sacrifice and purity are stated as universal that apply to males alone; masculine plural imperatives abound throughout the book. Blessings are promised that would be contingent on the actions of men, yet the gender is not specified. For example, if Israel is obedient to the Lord, God says, "you shall give chase to your enemies, and they shall fall before you by the sword. Five of you shall give chase to a hundred, and a hundred of you shall give chase to ten thousand" (26:7–8): since women were not enrolled in the army, clearly this is addressing only males, yet the focus on men is never identified, because the male is the implied normative subject throughout. Apart from the obvious harm that androcentrism does to those of genders other than male in a culture, androcentrism is destructive to males because it reinforces the assumption that their experiences and perspectives are normative and worthy of authority. This can result in men developing drastically distorted understandings of their personal agency, the importance of their bodies and desires, and the inevitability of their social authority.

A third subject constructed by Leviticus is the one whose lived experiences are ignored or marginalized. The ancient believers who are lesbian or gay, sex workers whose economic precarity keeps them engaged in practices that entail their social abjection; enslaved Canaanites facing a future of endless labor with no hope of being freed—all these wait silently in the shadows of the book of Leviticus, their bodies and spirits not accounted for in the honoring of covenantal relationship. The Israelite ritual system doubtless offered stability, joy, and powerful experiences of the divine to countless ancient believers. But just as surely, its androcentrism presented women and genderqueer or non-normative masculine persons with a limited and harmful set of choices. They had been formed and sustained by their culture with its understandings of theological truth, ethics, and communal memory, yet their gendered identity was ignored or punitively regulated. For readers committed to cherishing these texts as sacred, awareness of this can be extraordinarily painful. In response, women must map their own identity somehow onto the idealized male subject, perhaps seeking validation from actual male authority figures, trying to hear themselves as addressed despite the inevitable cognitive dissonance, or striving valiantly to ignore the psychic and social aggression in their culture's distortion of the experiences of those who are not cisgender heterosexual males. Alternatively, a feminist hermeneutic will assist them in acknowledging that their subjectivity has been misunderstood and disrespected, and they can take up a creative posture of resistance.

Conflict in Leviticus may be viewed through laws intended to regulate and resolve disputes in the holy community. Integrity in witness is a value prized by ancient Israel as a communal obligation, something that may be adduced in support of feminist work to make known the harms and distortions of patriarchy. Those who have knowledge of a matter are expected to testify (Lev 5:1). Deceit, robbery, fraud, and false testimony are to be punished (6:2–7; 19:11–13). Mockery and obstruction of those with visual or hearing impairment are not to be tolerated (19:14). Unjust judges, slanderers, mercenaries, those who hate others or seek vengeance, and those who exploit resident aliens will face justice (19:15–18, 33); honest trade practices are expected (19:35–36). These parameters for mutual accountability constitute excellent norms in every age, if they are accompanied by a nuanced understanding about what can drive desperate people to malfeasance. Systemic inequities can collude in creating crises within which criminal choices and other undesirable behaviors take place. Feminist interpreters may explore these norms, along with their intended and unintended consequences, along traditional avenues of theological and ethical inquiry. Feminists may also amplify the possibilities represented by these values and juridical processes within newer theoretical frameworks for gender justice and racial equity that could not have been anticipated by the ancient scribes.

Covenant in Leviticus interweaves orthodox theological belief, remembrance of Israel's history, and pragmatic observance of the statutes and ordinances of the Law. The God who redeemed Israel from slavery in Egypt requires the trust and obedience of this covenant people and sanctifies them; right theology is essential. "I am the Lord" is offered over fifty times as justification for the ritual practices and regulations of Leviticus (see 11:44, 45; 18:4, 5, and *passim*). The repeated refrain makes clear that honoring the deity lies at the heart of halakhic observance. Israel must remember, too, that they have flourished in freedom due to the Lord's saving actions on their behalf. Thus obedience is itself an offering to the God who compelled Pharaoh to release them so that they could worship. The observances commanded in Leviticus may be seen—notwithstanding the flaws and challenges that they present feminist interpretation on particular topics—as a holistic way of understanding lived experience in the presence of the Holy.

NUMBERS

The book of Numbers opens with a view of the military configuration of Israel as a holy-war camp. Moses and Aaron take a census of the male warriors according to tribe and clan. The Lord gives specifications for the deployment of regiments and their companies, the handling of the tabernacle with its furnishing and utensils, and procedures for ensuring the purification and moral integrity of the camp. Leaders of the Israelite tribes present offerings, and the holy-war camp sets out. Numbers pays close attention to details such as the names of individuals, the material specifics of offerings that are brought to the altar, the order in which the different contingents set out and encamp, the precise itinerary they pursue (33:1–49), and future territory boundaries and other specifics of allotments in Canaan (34:1—35:15). This kind of narration gives the impression of historical accuracy, though the picture rendered is in fact idealized. Such detailed narration may also serve to illustrate a theological point: that the ordered structure of Israel's camp and scrupulous adherence to divine commands perfectly reflects the divine will. Priestly narration of divine commands and their flawless execution in the book of Joshua will make a similar point. Resistant readers may note the feminist insight that ostensibly natural authoritative discourses, with their heavy reliance on numbers and other quantifiable features, can veil ideologies the merits of which are far from empirically verifiable.

Several passages in Numbers are of particular interest for feminist interpretation. One case law requires that a married woman suspected of adultery undergo the abhorrent practice of trial by ordeal, drinking a toxic libation in hopes that lack of harm will "prove" her innocence

(Numbers 5). Miriam and Aaron contest a decision of Moses to marry an outsider ("a Cushite woman," Num 12:1), the wrath of the Lord burns against them, and Miriam alone is punished. Miriam had stood watch over her infant brother Moses (Exod 2:4) and had led the celebration of Israel's deliverance at the Red Sea (Exod 15:20–21). Her punishment here—spontaneous skin disease and a week of banishment from the Israelite camp—renders this Israelite heroine as abject, in the sense made famous by theorist Julia Kristeva: cast out of a social system (literally or metaphorically) as dangerously impure, contagious, or revolting. Her skin contagion in this case is meant to signal her rebuke by the Lord.

Fruitful for feminist analysis are a set of complaint narratives in the Pentateuch in which the Israelites become fearful or resentful during their journey through the wilderness and protest bitterly. God's response varies—benevolent provision or brutal punishment could come from the deity, apparently depending on whether the complaint was considered reasonable or not. Immediately after having crossed the Red Sea, the Israelites had contended against Moses and Aaron because of the dearth of food and lack of fresh water (Exod 15:22—17:7). Through divine intervention, brackish water had been made potable, manna had appeared on the ground each morning, and water had streamed from a rock struck by Moses. This model of divine responsiveness to human need can sustain and ground feminist work for healing and justice. Gender and sexual minorities, the poor, those subjugated on racial or ethnic grounds, and others caught in wildernesses of intersectional oppression may look to feminist readings of the Exodus complaint stories as validation of political protest and the naming of human need. But here in Numbers, the divine response to Israelite complaints is markedly different. A general observation undercuts the viability of protest ("when the people complained in the hearing of the Lord about their misfortunes, the Lord heard it and his anger was kindled. Then the fire of the Lord burned against them, and consumed some outlying parts of the camp," Num 11:1). Such a text could profitably be resisted by feminists. Taken as symbolic, it suggests that those unhappy with the status quo may not raise their voices without risking punitive action, here divine wrath that consumes the liminal or "outlying" parts of the communal space, forcing inhabitants to move toward the center—toward uniformity and docility—in order to survive. Some then complain about the manna, craving meat instead. The Lord's wrathful response is to flood the camp with quails and then, while the people are eating, to strike them with a massive plague (11:4–33). When the people give voice to overwhelming fear about Canaanite enemies ahead and allow their fear to fuel the hope to return to Egypt, it is framed as rebellion, refusal to believe in God's power, and testing God (14:9, 11, 22). The infuriated deity swears that none of the current generation except Caleb and Joshua will enter Canaan: "your dead bodies will fall in this wilderness. And your children shall be shepherds in this wilderness for forty years, and shall suffer for your faithlessness, until the last of your dead bodies lies in the wilderness" (14:32–33). As with other stories of divinely ordained extermination of thousands of God's own people, these narrations of divine wrath should give feminist readers pause. Theology based on brutal suppression is better analyzed as a distorted reflection of the cruel operations of patriarchy in history than as something appropriate to assert about the Creator who redeems and sustains the vulnerable.

In the rebellion of Korah the Levite against Moses and Aaron (Numbers 16), we glimpse a fascinating theopolitical dispute about the status of priestly leaders. Korah's anti-hierarchy position is roundly rejected by the biblical narrator, who has Korah, his confederates Dathan and Abiram, and their families swallowed by the earth so that they go down, alive and screaming, to Sheol (16:31–34). But Korah's perspective may be compelling to resistant readers of feminist sensibility: "All the congregation are holy, every one of them, and the Lord is among them! So why then do you exalt yourselves above the assembly of the Lord?" (Num 16:3).

In Numbers 25, the zeal of the Israelite hero Phinehas dramatically obliterates the risks of cultural difference. Israelite men become sexually involved with Moabite women; in the imagination of ancient scribes, such fraternizing could lead to idolatry and worse, so the narrative continues with an enraged YHWH having the chiefs of the people impaled, then sending a plague that kills twenty-four thousand Israelites. Phinehas impales an Israelite man and Midianite woman in the act of intercourse to underline the importance of dedication to the stricture against mixing with foreign peoples; he is rewarded with a perpetual "covenant of peace" (25:12). Feminist commentators have much to say about ways in which female bodies generally, and the sexuality of outsider females in particular, are construed in texts such as Numbers 25. Phallocentric Priestly and

Deuteronomic traditions betray a hyperbolic cultural anxiety about women. In the Pentateuch and beyond, female bodies are constructed as lures that could tempt the faithful Israelite male into catastrophic error that could destroy the social fabric of Israel.

A story in Numbers 27:1–10 has drawn the attention of feminist readers. Five daughters of a Manassite named Zelophehad ask to be permitted to receive their father's inheritance, given the absence of any brothers to stake a competing claim; Moses allows it. Some feminist interpreters cite this text as actual or metaphorical precedent for a hermeneutic of generosity and compassion, using the story as a license for creative work that moves beyond existing juridical constraints. Others would object that the anomalous nature of the case presented by the daughters of Zelophehad serves only to underscore the profound disenfranchisement of Israelite women that functions as the uninterrogated central norm. It is worth noting that the daughters of Zelophehad are later required to marry within their father's clan so (male) control of their inherited wealth can ensure that it stays within appropriate patrilineal bounds (Numbers 36).

DEUTERONOMY

The figure of the prophet Moses towers over Deuteronomy. The opening chapters of the book are framed as a speech in which the leader rehearses the moments of grace and struggle that have formed this people during their journey "through all that great and terrible wilderness" (Deut 1:19) to the boundary of Canaan. The historical retrospective is presented as the official story, the authoritative rendering of the community's experience. Feminists have learned to examine, contest, and amplify this sort of narration. Official versions of history purport to identify all of the formative events and persons of influence who matter—yet the authorized histories inevitably leave out ambiguous moments and contestatory interpretations, distorting experiences and silencing dissent, suppressing alternate versions of the shared history that might highlight truths not malleable to the authority's ideological purposes. Deuteronomy is an elegant and stirring piece of ancient rhetoric. It is also a relentlessly androcentric, militarized framing of Israel's identity that articulates in the strongest terms a theological portrayal of the Lord as one who punishes covenant infractions without mercy.

In the case laws in Deuteronomy 12–26, feminist interpreters may consider two particular statutes that illustrate the operations of patriarchy, understood as a distorted system of masculinist privilege that deploys power to ensure filial compliance in social and political terms. First, the case of the "stubborn and rebellious son" (21:18–21) regulates insubordination on the part of a youth within his own family as an offense that merits capital punishment. Noncompliance and heedlessness—essentially ignoring the discipline leveled by parental authority figures—are perceived as threatening the social fabric of the entire community. The offender must be obliterated through execution: the son is to be taken out and stoned to death. The fear-based logic of this homicidal patriarchalism is claimed as strategically effective for governance: "So you shall purge the evil from your midst; and all Israel will hear, and be afraid" (21:21). A second case law that has drawn feminist attention showcases cultural bias in favor of the male in the matter of divorce, which may be initiated unilaterally by a husband on entirely subjective grounds (24:1). A wife has no reciprocal rights in this regard. The law allows for women to be cast into economic peril at the whim of a displeased husband.[9] The legislating of harm in these two case laws, which may be theorized as iconic gestures reflecting a larger cultural politics, demonstrates the dynamics of domination and ideological control on which patriarchal polities are based.

There are numerous life-giving aspects of the theology and rhetoric of Deuteronomy to be explored and celebrated in feminist analysis. Feminist constructive theology may draw on the stipulation that God not be represented in any idol, figure, or image (4:15–18). "Since you saw no form when the Lord spoke to you at Horeb out of the fire, take care and watch yourselves closely, so that you do not act corruptly by making an idol for yourselves, in the form of any figure" (4:15–16): this may serve as a powerful resource for countering the insistent androcentrism of representations of the Holy in many theological and cultural contexts. The agricultural bounty of the land envisioned in Deuteronomy may be read as a symbol of the abundance of life lived in loving relationship with the God who redeems the oppressed. First interrogating the underlying ideological script about militarized expropriation of Canaanite territory, the feminist may perform a creative rereading that frames this compelling

9. Judith Plaskow writes, "True, the rabbis were aware of the harshness of certain laws pertaining to women and sought to mitigate their effects. . . . But the framework that necessitated such mitigations went unquestioned. Women's Otherness was left intact. The Jewish passion for justice did not extend to Jewish women" (*Standing Again at Sinai*, 5).

vision of abundance as true *shalom* for all: "The Lord your God is bringing you into a good land, a land with flowing streams, with springs and underground waters welling up in valleys and hills, a land of wheat and barley, of vines and fig trees and pomegranates, a land of olive trees and honey, a land where you may eat bread without scarcity, where you will lack nothing" (8:7–9). Deuteronomy's care for the poor is radical; the exhortation to "Open your hand to the poor and needy neighbor in your land" (15:11) could energize ongoing feminist efforts to transform the economic inequities that create misery across the globe. Those who see feminist work in prophetic terms may be emboldened by Deuteronomy's promise that God will continually raise up prophets for truth-telling and visionary leadership (18:15–18); this text may be taken to secure the credentials of feminist, womanist, and queer "prophets like Moses" who speak new subversive truths within their communities.

Finally, the Shema, "Hear, O Israel: The Lord is our God, the Lord alone. You shall love the Lord your God with all your heart, and with all your soul, and with all your might" (6:4–5), calls believers to focus their fidelity on the Holy One. No other source of power can redeem and sustain. On the logic that harm perpetrated against creatures or the created order mocks the Creator, the feminist might use this exhortation as holy ground on which to stand while dismantling pernicious political structures, opposing social injustice, and envisioning new forms of sacred community.

FOR FURTHER READING

Brenner, Athalya, ed. *A Feminist Companion to Exodus to Deuteronomy.* FCB, Second Series. Sheffield: Sheffield Academic, 1994.

——, ed. *A Feminist Companion to Genesis.* FCB, Second Series. Sheffield: Sheffield Academic, 1998.

Claassens, L. Juliana M. *Claiming Her Dignity: Female Resistance in the Old Testament.* Collegeville, MN: Liturgical, 2016.

Drinkwater, Gregg, Joshua Lesser, and David Shneer, eds. *Torah Queeries: Weekly Commentaries on the Hebrew Bible.* New York: New York University Press, 2012.

Junior, Nyasha. *An Introduction to Womanist Biblical Interpretation.* Louisville: Westminster John Knox, 2015.

Newsom, Carol A., Sharon H. Ringe, and Jacqueline E. Lapsley, eds. *The Women's Bible Commentary*. 3rd anniversary ed. Louisville: Westminster John Knox, 2012.

Plaskow, Judith. *Standing Again at Sinai: Judaism from a Feminist Perspective*. New York: HarperCollins, 1990.

Scholz, Susanne. *Introducing the Women's Hebrew Bible*. Introductions in Feminist Theology 13. New York: T&T Clark, 2007.

Schüssler Fiorenza, Elisabeth. *Wisdom Ways: Introducing Feminist Biblical Interpretation*. Maryknoll, NY: Orbis, 2001.

Stone, Ken. "Marriage and Sexual Relations in the World of the Hebrew Bible." In *The Oxford Handbook of Theology, Sexuality, and Gender*, edited by Adrian Thatcher, 173–88. Oxford: Oxford University Press, 2015.

Yee, Gale A. *Poor Banished Children of Eve: Woman as Evil in the Hebrew Bible*. Minneapolis: Fortress Press, 2003.

PART II

The Deuteronomistic History

2.

Intersections of Ethnicity, Gender, Sexuality, and Nation

VANESSA LOVELACE

FEMINIST AND INTERSECTIONAL PERSPECTIVES IN THE DEUTERONOMISTIC HISTORY

The Deuteronomistic Narrative or History (DH) is an academic term for a collection of books that comprise Deuteronomy and Joshua, Judges, Samuel, and Kings (the Former Prophets in the Hebrew canon). The DH covers the history of Israel from the late Mosaic period in the book of Deuteronomy to the conquest of the land of Canaan, and ends with the destruction of Judah and Jerusalem and the elite Judahites taken captive to Babylon. Martin Noth coined the term DH based on his theory that this body of literature formed a single literary unity composed by a single author living in exile (sixth century BCE), whom Noth referred to as the Deuteronomist (Dtr).[1] He based his claim on the recognition that the collection shared language, style, and theology similar to Deuteronomy. The central theological thread running through the DH is the covenantal relationship between YHWH and Israel. YHWH promised them land, fertility, and security as long as the people kept the covenantal obligations, and the loss of it all if they failed. According to Dtr, the

---

1. See Martin Noth, *The Deuteronomistic History*, JSOTSup (Sheffield: JSOT Press, 1981). Although Noth believed in a single author, a number of scholars agree that more than one writer/editor was responsible for the body of work, but speak of Dtr in the singular. I am following that practice here.

Babylonian exile was divine retribution for Israel's long history of disobedience.

Theodore Mullen reflects the general consensus among biblical scholars that the writer or writers of the DH were members of the elite class, perhaps the priestly class, who composed the DH from "archaic originals" written in response to the threatened assimilation and ethnic dissolution of the exiled community. Mullen maintained that the DH functioned to establish ethnic boundaries based on shared memories of a common history:

> Within the context of the crisis produced by the destruction of the Judahite state, the traditions of the past were assembled in a way that would provide for the continued survival of the people who would constitute "Israel." The possibility of using this as a starting point for interpreting the deuteronomistic history is strongly supported by one clear datum: emerging from the exile in Babylon was an ethnic community that identified itself as Judahite/Israelite and asserted its identity with those communities that had preceded it and from which its members claimed to be direct and "legitimate" descendants.[2]

Thus, despite the categorization of the DH as "history," it is less a historical work in the modern sense of a dispassionate report on dates and events, than theological and ideological revisions and additions to received traditions. Mullen's insights from his use of socio-scientific methods help the reader to understand the ways in which biblical writers used Israel's past traditions to construct an Israelite identity during the exile. Mullen and other scholars frequently cite the work of social anthropologist Fredrik Barth and historian and political scientist Benedict Anderson.[3] Barth argued that despite mobility, social interaction, and shared information, ethnic groups are defined not by the "cultural stuff" they have in common but by their ability to establish and maintain the boundaries that distinguish one group

---

2. E. Theodore Mullen Jr., *Narrative History and Ethnic Boundaries: The Deuteronomistic Historian and the Creation of Israelite National Identity* (Atlanta: Scholars, 1993), 14.

3. See for example Mark G. Brett, ed., *Ethnicity and the Bible* (Leiden: E. J. Brill, 1996); Kenton Sparks, *Ethnicity and Identity in Ancient Israel: Prolegomena to the Study of Ethnic Sentiments and Their Expression in the Hebrew Bible* (Winona Lake, IN: Eisenbrauns, 1998); and Mark Vessey, Sharon V. Betcher, Robert A. Daum, and Harry O. Maier, eds., *The Calling of the Nations: Exegesis, Ethnography and Empire in a Biblical-Historical Present* (Toronto: Toronto University Press, 2011).

from another, regardless of their shared geographical territory.[4] Likewise, Anderson contends that nations are socially constructed entities rather than natural, organically occurring ones with ties to a geographic location or history. Therefore, for Anderson the nation is "an imagined political community" that arises from a community's sense of shared experience and identity. However, it is also limited because its members operate out of a sense of exclusiveness.[5]

Israel's identity is certainly defined by its exclusiveness from other nations.[6] However, what is often missing from theories of nation is an analysis of the role of gender in the process. Feminist theorists such as Anne McClintock argue that all nationalisms are gendered. The intersection of gender and nation must be explored, beginning with the assertion that nations have historically amounted to the sanctioned institutionalization of gender *difference*: "All too often in male nationalisms, gender difference between women and men serves to symbolically define the limits of national difference and power between men."[7] Sociologists Floya Anthias and Nira Yuval-Davis identify several ways women affect and are affected by national and ethnic processes: as biological reproducers of members of ethnic collectivities; as reproducers of the boundaries of ethnic or national groups; as central participants in the ideological reproduction of the collectivity and as transmitters of its culture; as symbolic signifiers of national difference; and as participants in national, economic, political, and military struggles.[8]

An example of a feminist biblical scholar's use of this methodological approach is Erin Runions's analysis of the intersection of gender and nation in the particular formation of an Israelite identity. In her reading of the book of Micah, Runions

4. Fredrik Barth, "Introduction," in *Ethnic Groups and Boundaries* (Boston: Little, Brown, 1969), 15–16.

5. Benedict Anderson, *Imagined Communities: Reflections on the Origin and Spread of Nationalism* (London: Verso, 1983), 49. Anderson stresses that "imagined" should not be taken to mean "fabrication" or "falsity," as Ernest Gellner does in his assessment of nationalism, but rather as in "imagining" and "creating."

6. Some social scientists believe the term *nation* is a modern concept that does not apply to ancient societies. For a defense of the biblical roots of the modern nation, see Mira Morgenstern's *Conceiving a Nation: The Development of Political Discourse in the Hebrew Bible* (University Park: Pennsylvania State University Press, 2009).

7. Anne McClintock, "'No Longer in a Future Heaven': Race, Gender and Nationalism," in *Dangerous Liaisons*, ed. Anne McClintock, Aamir Mufti, and Elai Shohat (Minneapolis: University of Minnesota Press, 1997), 89.

8. Floya Anthias and Nira Yuval-Davis, *Racialized Boundaries: Race, Nation, Gender,Colour and Class and the Anti-Racist Struggle* (New York: Routledge, 1992), 115.

critiques interpretations of the covenantal relationship between YHWH and Israel that rely on dominant gender binary constructions. She contends that such readings impose heterosexual ideals on Israel's identity and future, as when discourse on Israel's theological identity renders the nation of Israel as a "suffering penitent woman, punished, passively waiting for rescue and led into glory over the nations by Yahweh," the divine male hero.[9] In addition to conveying the unequal covenantal relationship between YHWH and Israel metaphorically in gendered terms, the intersection of ethnicity, gender, and sexuality in the DH is demonstrated in a number of ways, to include the portrayal of sexual relations with foreign women as a threat to Israel's identity, the feminization of foreign men, and violence against women as a means for constructing the ideal Israelite masculinity.

THE BOOK OF JOSHUA: ESTABLISHING AND MAINTAINING BOUNDARIES

The book of Joshua is situated between the instructions in Deuteronomy for how to live in the land promised to the people of Israel by YHWH, and life in the settled land in Judges after having conquered the territory. Joshua is about establishing ethnic boundary markers, literal and symbolic. On one hand, it is about the Israelites crossing the geographical borders east of the Jordan River to take possession of Canaan on the other side. On the other hand, it is about establishing and maintaining symbolic boundary markers that distinguish the Israelite "us" from the Canaanite "them." As stated by L. Daniel Hawk, "The impulse to fix and maintain these boundaries drives the story from start to finish, interweaving themes of land, behavior, and ethnicity into an intricate tapestry."[10]

The themes of land, behavior, and ethnicity intersect with gender, sexuality, and religion. For example, the invasion of the land is depicted as the sexual violation of a woman. Socially approved gender constructs define what it means to be a good Israelite, and the exclusive boundary maintenance is over against exogamy, marrying outside the lineage. In Joshua, this is carried out in a three-part directive authorized by Israel's deity in the book of Deuteronomy:

9. Erin Runions, *Changing Subjects: Gender, Nation and Future in Micah* (Sheffield: Sheffield Academic, 2001), 201.

10. L. Daniel Hawk, *Joshua*, Berit Olam (Collegeville, MN: Liturgical, 2000), xi.

utterly destroy the indigenous people of the land of Canaan, refrain from entering into treaties with them, and ban intermarrying with them (Deut 7:1–3). Given that interethnic social interaction is necessary in order to establish who belongs and who is excluded as a member of Israel, Dtr needs the Canaanites to define the Israelites. Therefore, Dtr resolves this conundrum by explaining that the Canaanites remained in the land as a result of the people's disobedience. Still, the idea that Israel is instructed to completely wipe out the indigenous population—whether or not it really happened—with YHWH's approval, is troublesome.[11] As Hawk asserts, "The establishment of national identity is thus associated with a program of violence against other peoples, one that is sanctioned and sanctified by divine edict."[12]

CANAANITE WOMEN AS SYMBOLIC BORDERS

The invasion of the land and the command to "utterly destroy" the inhabitants of Canaan (Deut 7:2) belong to the sphere of masculine performativity, where, for example, men are said to engage in violent behavior as part of their male gender identity.[13] To this extent, Ovidiu Creangă rightly refers to the book of Joshua as an androcentric text.[14] Women are seldom mentioned in Joshua; in fact, on the occasions where they would be expected, such as the welcoming of the returning warriors with songs and dances of victory (e.g., Miriam in Exod 15:21 and Jephthah's daughter in Judges 11), the women are absent.[15] Therefore, it might not come as a surprise that there is not an abundance of feminist and womanist treatments of Joshua, with the exception of the character Rahab and

11. A number of scholars question the conquest model of Israel's origins in Canaan and offer alternative proposals, to include a gradual migration model and an internal social upheaval model.

12. Hawk, *Joshua*, xii.

13. See Judith Butler's *Gender Trouble: Feminism and the Subversion of Identity* (New York: Routledge, 1990), where she introduces the theory of "gender performativity," a term that she coined to argue that gender roles are performed rather than biologically determined.

14. Ovidiu Creangă, "Variations on the Theme of Masculinity: Joshua's Gender In/Stability in the Conquest Narrative (Josh. 1–12)," in *Men and Masculinity in the Hebrew Bible and Beyond*, ed. Ovidiu Creangă (Sheffield: Sheffield Phoenix, 2010), 83.

15. Ovidiu Creangă, "The Silenced Songs of Victory: Power, Gender and Memory in the Conquest Narrative of Joshua (Joshua 1–12)," in *A Question of Sex? Gender and Difference in the Hebrew Bible and Beyond*, ed. Deborah W. Rooke, Hebrew Bible Monographs 14 (Sheffield: Sheffield Phoenix, 2007), 106–23.

to a lesser degree Achsah.[16] Nevertheless, women not only are present in the text but figure in the establishment and maintenance of Israel's ethnic boundaries as geographical space and physical bodies. Political scientist Julie Mostov writes of the gendering of boundaries and spaces (landscapes, farmlands, and battlefields) as feminine in national mythology (songs, poetry, and literature). According to Mostov, male warriors are assigned subject positions as invaders acquiring territory and possessions: "It is over and through the feminine body that they pursue these goals. They forge their identities as males, as agents of the nation, over the symbolic and physical territory of the feminine 'homeland.'"[17]

The Hebrew Bible prophets speak metaphorically of cities and territory as women endangered or sexually violated by alien invaders in the context of warfare. In Hebrew, both cities and land are grammatically gendered as feminine. Therefore, the land is the first "woman" to appear in the book of Joshua. However, there are real women in the land, who symbolically stand for the nation. Therefore, the rape and murder of the Canaanite women also represent the erasure and replacement of the ethnic other.[18] As V. Spike Petersen explains, "The rape of the body/nation not only violates frontiers but disrupts—by planting alien seed or destroying reproductive viability—the maintenance of the community through time."[19]

If rape of the enemy's women produces the invader's children, then intermarriage has the opposite effect. Dora Mbuwayesango explains that exogamy puts at risk the special status of the people of Israel as YHWH's elect. She writes that, "Intermarriage, specifically between Israelite males and Canaanite women, will lead to corruption and loss of this unique identity and status."[20] More specifically, intermarriage will contaminate the purity of the Israelite *men*. Although English

16. For example, Athalya Brenner's popular Feminist Companion to the Bible series that includes commentary on Exodus to Deuteronomy and Samuel to Kings skips over the book of Joshua.

17. Julie Mostov, "'Our Women'/'Their Women': Symbolic Boundaries, Territorial Markers, and Violence in the Balkans," *Peace & Change* 20, no. 4 (October 1995): 522.

18. Simone de Beauvoir introduced the idea of "the other" and the verb "to other" to explain the process of constructing one's own identity in opposition to the Other as both mutual and unequal identities in *The Second Sex*, 1st American ed., trans. Constance Borde and Sheila Malovany-Chevallier (New York: Alfred A. Knopf, 2010).

19. V. Spike Petersen, "Gendered Nationalism: Reproducing 'Us' versus 'Them,'" *Peace Review* 6 (March 1994): 4.

20. Dora Mbuwayesango, "Canaanite Women and Israelite Women in Deuteronomy: The Intersection of Sexism and Imperialism," in *Postcolonial Interventions: Essays in Honor of R. S. Sugirtharajah*, ed. Tat-Siong Benny Liew (Sheffield: Sheffield Phoenix, 2009), 48–49.

translations of the Hebrew verb *hoten* is "to marry" or "to intermarry," in its verbal denominative form in Deuteronomy 7:3 the subject is male and literally means "to make oneself a daughter's husband, bridegroom, or son-in-law." Therefore, although the edict warns of both giving and taking of women in marriage, the Canaanite women are seen as a threat to the nation of Israel, who would seduce the men of Israel into worshiping their deities. As such, Israel's deity orders Joshua to command his men not only to avoid sexual relations with Canaanite women but also to totally destroy them in order to maintain Israel's ethnic boundaries.

MASCULINE PERFORMATIVITY IN JOSHUA

From the preparations for war to the conquest and its aftermath, masculine performativity by men is on full display in Joshua. As David Clines and others have demonstrated, to be a warrior is an essential male characteristic in the Hebrew Bible.[21] Joshua and his men perform their roles by arming themselves, consecrating themselves, and circumcising themselves, among other undertakings. While the women, children, and livestock are told to remain behind in the Transjordan region (Josh 1:14), the men are instructed to take up arms in preparation to conquer Canaan on the other side of the Jordan River. The day before the invasion, Joshua commands the men to sanctify themselves, "for tomorrow the Lord will do wonders among you" (3:5). Although the command is addressed to *ha-'am*, "the people," the events in Joshua recall the preparations at Mt. Sinai when Moses readied the people to receive the covenant at the end of a three-day encampment (Exod 19:14–15). After Moses consecrated the people and they washed their clothes (v. 14), he told them "do not go near a woman" (v. 15). The prohibition against engaging in sexual relations with a woman signifies that men are the addressees. The military context of Joshua 3:5 would imply that it is the troops preparing to enter Canaan who require ritual purity, ostensibly by abstaining from sexual contact with women (cf. 1 Sam 21:4).

If there is any doubt remaining as to whether the people in Joshua 3:5 are the male members, YHWH's command to Joshua to

21. For a treatment of masculinity in the Hebrew Bible see, for example, David J. A. Clines, "David the Man: The Construction of Masculinity in the Hebrew Bible," in *Interested Parties: The Ideology of Writers and Readers of the Hebrew Bible*, JSOTsup 205; Gender, Culture, Theory, 1 (Sheffield: Sheffield Academic, 1995), 212–41.

circumcise the Israelites (Heb. lit. "sons of Israel") once they have entered Canaan (5:2–9) should disabuse the reader of such thoughts. Circumcision is a sign of participation in the covenant between Abraham and Israel's deity and denotes membership in the nation of Israel (Gen 17:14). It is performed on the male members and therefore is also a sign of masculinity. This has led many scholars to argue that male members of the community are the normative Israelites, while women are subsumed among the male members as daughters and wives. L. A. Hoffman states that "circumcision was a rite of masculine status bestowal in which one man, the father, initiates a man-to-be, his son, into the covenant with God (conceived as a man)."[22]

DEVOTE TO DESTRUCTION

Many scholars have raised the moral problem of the Conquest Narrative in Joshua. The command given to Moses in Deuteronomy 6:2 (cf. 20:16–18) that every living thing, human or animal, was "to be devoted to the Lord for destruction" is repeated by Joshua (Josh 6:17) just prior to the fall of Jericho. The deuteronomistic writer viewed the ritual practice of putting one's enemies to death as an act of consecrating them to YHWH as "ban" or *herem* in Hebrew (vv. 21–25). This was YHWH's expected response from Israel for choosing them from among the nations. Walter Brueggemann asserts that "violence is intrinsic to the status of chosenness, for the land to be *given* is the land to be *taken*, as is required."[23] However, it is not the bloodshed as a result of taking the land that is morally objectionable for some readers. Rather, it is that the violent seizure of the land and destruction of all inhabitants are endorsed by Israel's deity, who goes before Israel as the divine warrior.

While the conquest narrative of God delivering the Israelites from slavery in Egypt might be lifted up as a story of liberation for marginalized and oppressed peoples, Robert Warrior, a member of the Osage Nation of American Indians, presents an alternative perspective. He notes that the covenant between YHWH and Israel must be read from the two sides of deliverance and conquest. If one is

---

22. Cited in John Goldingay, "The Significance of Circumcision," *JSOT* 25, no. 88 (June 2000): 4.

23. Walter Brueggemann, "The God of Joshua: An Ambivalent Field of Negotiation," in *Joshua and Judges*, ed. Athalya Brenner and Gale A. Yee, Texts @ Contexts series (Minneapolis: Fortress Press, 2013), 15 (emphasis original).

reading as a Native American who identifies with the Canaanites in the story, then the God of liberation, who commands the Israelites to "mercilessly annihilate the indigenous population," becomes the God of conquest in the victim's eyes.[24]

There is at least one exception to the ban. The story of Rahab the Canaanite in Joshua 2 interrupts the report of the impending seizure of the city of Jericho. Joshua sends two spies to reconnoiter the city. They spend the night at the residence of Rahab, who is sexualized as the proprietor or woman of a "house of promiscuity" (Josh 2:1). In colloquial speech, she runs a "house of ill repute," "brothel," or "whorehouse." Rahab refuses to obey a command from her king to turn the spies over to him. Instead, she lies about their whereabouts and hides them, while sending the king's men on a futile search for the two. In return for her generosity, she secures from them an agreement to deal kindly with her and her family by sparing their lives when they successfully invade the city, which she appears to have foreseen: "I know that the Lord has given you the land, and that dread of you has fallen on us, and that all the inhabitants of the land melt in fear before you" (2:9).

L. Daniel Hawk asserts that her concluding praise of YHWH "dresses Rahab in Israelite garb. She knows the songs Israel sings, can recount Israel's history, and acclaims Israel's God."[25] Ovidiu Creangă contends that Rahab's performance puts her in a position reserved for male leaders in Israel. He asserts that since the commemoration of Israel's past in the conquest narrative is an ideal masculine trait, "When Rahab returns to Israel's past in Josh. 2.9–11, she certainly undermines many of the narrative's assumptions about the privileged position of Israel's male leaders to recall their past."[26] Both of these comments infer that the writer has made Rahab's character out to be a "cross-dresser," both by putting her in Israelite attire and making her perform as an Israelite male to save her life and the lives of her family members. However, rather than her performance undermining the narrative's assumptions about masculinity in Joshua, as Creangă contends, it reinscribes stereotypes about foreign women as masculine.

Once Rahab and her family are safely ensconced beyond the walls of Jericho, the ban or devotion to destruction of everyone and

---

24. Robert Warrior, "Canaanites, Cowboys, and Indians," *USQR* 59, no. 1–2 (2005): 3, 6.
25. Hawk, *Joshua*, 45.
26. Creangă, "Silenced Songs," 108.

everything within the walls commences. Joshua and his men set aside items made of silver and gold and bronze and iron for the treasury of the house of YHWH as part of the ban (Josh 6:19, 24) and burn down the city. Next on the itinerary is the city of Ai. However, rather than a repeat of events as they took place at Jericho, the Israelites experience their first defeat. The narrator informs the reader that a certain Achan has violated the directive and kept some of the devoted things for himself. His actions anger YHWH, who prevents Israel from capturing and destroying the city of Ai. Their failure causes their hearts to melt in fear and the soldiers turn their backs to the enemy in retreat (Josh 7:4–9). According to Creangă, the construction of the gendered subject in the Deuteronomic law of warfare relegates women to a "secondary status (penetrated) in relation to 'man' (penetrator)."[27] Put another way, the defeated are feminine and the victors are masculine. Therefore, when the men of Israel turn and run in fear of the men of Ai, they put themselves in the feminine position of being penetrated. One man's disobedience threatens the masculinity of all the men of Israel.

All Israel is blamed for the violation despite Achan being the offender (7:1). Therefore, the entire community has now come under the ban. The only way to remove the blight is to destroy the stolen items. Achan, his wife and family, his entire household, and livestock are killed, burned with their possessions, and stones are heaped upon their remains (7:24–26). YHWH is appeased and emboldens Joshua to go up against the city of Ai and its king and put all the inhabitants to the sword as they did to Jericho: "The total of those who fell that day, both men and women, was twelve thousand—all the people of Ai" (Josh 8:25). Yet, in contrast to Jericho, the ban only applies to the city's inhabitants; the men are now permitted to keep the spoils and livestock as booty for themselves (Josh 8:2b, 27).

Following the destruction of Ai, Joshua assembles all Israel for a reading of the book of the law at Mt. Ebal (Josh 8:30–35) to reiterate the conditions that must be met to remain a member of the covenant community. As previously mentioned, the phrase "all Israel" usually has meant all the male members of Israel eligible for military service. However, in Joshua 8, the women are again included as part of the covenant reading, as they were in Exodus 19: "There was not a word of all that Moses commanded that Joshua did not read before all the assembly of Israel, and the women, and the little ones, and the

27. Creangă, "Silenced Songs," 116.

aliens who resided among them" (Josh 8:35). The women's presence, on one level, reminds the assembled men of their role as defenders of women and their sexuality from outside invading forces. Men who fail in their duty are considered impotent. On another level, including the women reinforces their own obligations as signifiers of the national boundaries. Israelite women are not just passive symbols of the nation. As Musa Dube noted in her postcolonial interpretation of Joshua 1–12, "As women from the colonizer's side, Israelite women become the measure and keepers of the purity or holiness of their nation."[28]

DIVISION OF THE LAND

After the conquests, YHWH instructs Joshua to allot the territory to the tribes of Israel as an inheritance (Joshua 13–19). Each of the twelve tribes (except the priestly tribe of Levi) receives a portion of land. Yet, despite the religious element, Joshua and his men benefit materially from the conflicts. The men are rewarded with livestock and possessions in the form of booty, land, and even women. In a patriarchal society, fathers and husbands control their daughters' and wives' sexuality, a commodity to be sold or traded. When Caleb receives his portion of land, he offers to give his daughter Achsah as a wife to whoever would attack Kiriath-Sepher and take possession of it. Caleb's kinsman Othniel succeeds in conquering the city and takes Achsah for his wife (Josh 15:16). The author of the expression, "To the victor belongs the spoils" might not have had women in mind, but Sisera's mother in Judges 5 makes clear that women too are prizes to be won.[29]

As an aged Joshua's death draws near, he summons all the elders, heads, judges, and officers to encourage them to be steadfast in their obedience to the book of the law of Moses. Conceding the fact that they had not driven out all the nations in the land, he exhorts his male audience to swear their obedience to YHWH, lest they yield to the temptation to turn back and intermarry with the surviving inhabitants (23:12–13). He warns that YHWH will no longer remove

---

28. Musa Dube, *Postcolonial Feminist Interpretation of the Bible* (St. Louis: Chalice, 2000), 75.

29. The mother of the Canaanite general Sisera (Judg 5:30; cf. 4:7–16) sits anxiously at her window awaiting her son's return from battle, wondering, "Are they not finding and dividing the spoil?—A girl or two for every man; spoil of dyed stuffs for Sisera, spoil of dyed stuffs embroidered, two pieces of dyed work embroidered for my neck as spoil?"

the nations from the land and that the foreign wives would remain as a snare and trap for the Israelites. Just as Dtr earlier explained that the Canaanites remained on account of Israel's disobedience, here the writer uses the Canaanite women as justification for why YHWH took the land from Israel.

In a final deuteronomistic insertion, Joshua gathers the remainder of the tribes at Shechem for a covenant renewal ceremony (chap. 24). After recounting Israel's history and YHWH's graciousness toward the people, Joshua commands the people to choose between serving YHWH, the God their ancestors worshiped beyond the river, or the gods of the land. He makes clear his decision with the expression now commonly displayed in Christian homes: "but as for me and my household, we will serve the Lord" (Josh 24:15). The people swear to serve and obey YHWH only, and Joshua commemorates the event by setting up a stone at the site. After these things, Joshua dies (v. 29). The lesson of the book is clear: to be an insider is to demonstrate steadfast loyalty to YHWH; to disobey YHWH is to be an outsider.

THE BOOK OF JUDGES: THE CROSSING OF BOUNDARIES

Judges is a transitional book from the invasion of Canaan in the book of Joshua to the account of Israel's early settled life in the Promised Land prior to the monarchy. The book is named for the charismatic military leaders raised up by YHWH to deliver the Israelites from their enemies. The need for judges is characterized by Israel's cycle of disobedience. The people would rebel against YHWH and YHWH would give them into the hand of their enemies, who would oppress them. The people would cry out; YHWH would take pity on them and raise up judges to rescue them. After a period of rest, Israel would repeat the cycle, but even worse than before, creating a downward cycle into chaos. Despite the association of these figures in the modern reader's mind with robed figures administering justice from courtroom benches, only one figure, Deborah, judges Israel in the forensic sense of deciding disputes (Judg 4:5).

The prologue in Judges 1:1—2:5 makes clear why YHWH placed judges to rule over the people of Israel. Beginning with the announcement of Joshua's death, there is a theological retelling of the events in the book of Joshua concerning Israel's exploits in Canaan and an explanation why Israel was not able to rid the land of the Canaanites. The Israelites are accused of entering into treaties with the inhabitants and failing to tear down their altars. In the face of the current situation, Joshua's qualifying remarks in Joshua 23:11–13, that certain tribes could not drive out particular inhabitants, are warranted. They are reiterated in Judges 2:3, when a messenger of YHWH brings word of YHWH's disapproval: "So now I say, I will not drive them out before you; but they shall become adversaries to you, and their gods shall be a snare to you." Terry Brensinger contends that as such, "Israel's failure is not primarily the result of military or political incompetence," but rather is the people's inability to remain faithful to YHWH alone.[30]

What follows is an announcement that is reminiscent of Exodus 1:8, except rather than a new king rising in Egypt who did not know Joseph and the prosperity he brought, a generation arose in Israel that did not know YHWH (Judg 2:10). In contrast to their ancestors who witnessed YHWH's great works when they were brought up from Egypt and have since died, their descendants have no personal experience of YHWH. Therefore, the deuteronomistic evaluation, that "the Israelites did what was evil in the sight of the Lord" (2:11) mentioned throughout Judges (e.g., 3:7, 12; 4:1), does not come as a surprise. This assessment is an ominous sign that things will not go well for the people of Israel in the settlement period. If the book of Joshua was about establishing and maintaining boundaries, Judges is about what happens when the distinctions are blurred.

The Israelites' unsuccessful efforts to devote to destruction all the indigenous inhabitants of the land, brokering agreements with them and failing to tear down their altars, was from the perspective of Dtr a sign of the people's rejection of YHWH. The evil done by Israel is largely interpreted as the worship of other deities: "And they abandoned the Lord, and worshiped Baal and the Astartes" (Judg 2:1). While some might take for granted that apostasy was the cause of Israel's downfall, an analysis of the intersection of religion, ethnicity, and sexuality reveals a more cynical shift in Dtr's attribution of apostasy as the threat to Israel's identity. In Joshua 23, Joshua prohibits the Israelites from intermarrying with those who remained in the land. However, the women are never assigned direct blame for causing Israel to worship other gods. In contrast, Dtr makes a

---

30. Terry Brensinger, *Judges*, Believers Church Bible Commentary (Scottdale, PA: Herald, 1999), 35.

theological recalculation in Judges 3 and faults foreign women for Israel's turning from YHWH: "So the Israelites lived among the Canaanites, the Hittites, the Amorites, the Perizzites, the Hivites, and the Jebusites; and they took their daughters as wives for themselves, and their own daughters they gave to their sons; and they worshiped their gods" (Judg 3:5–6). As Amy Cottrill puts it, "The Israelites turn their women into outsiders, bring in foreign women as their own, and then conveniently blame these women for the nation's apostasy."[31]

THE INTERSECTION OF VIOLENCE AND GENDER

Nira Yuval-Davis maintains that "constructions of nationhood usually involve specific notions of both 'manhood' and 'womanhood.'"[32] To this point Judges offers an abundance of male and female characters to analyze how gender functions in the settlement period. In fact, Judges contains a larger number of named and unnamed female characters than in any other book in the Hebrew Bible. Nonetheless, the presence of so many women leaves little to celebrate as they are subjected to being sacrificed, kidnapped, raped, and murdered. Moreover, the construction of gender and ethnicity in Judges often renders foreign men as feminized and foreign women as masculinized.

The first judge raised up is Othniel, who is presented as a model judge. Following his death, there is the repeated relapse, oppression, lament, pity, deliverance, and rest. There is Ehud (Judg 3:11–29), then Shamgar (3:31), followed by a break in the usual course of events. Not only is the next charismatic leader a woman, but also YHWH is not said to have raised her up. Instead Deborah, the first woman to judge Israel, is given a deuteronomistic introduction as a woman, a prophet, wife of Lappidoth, and a judge. As a woman acting in the public sphere, commentators often consider her as having stepped outside the bounds of the traditional space reserved for women. Moreover, her role in delivering Israel is the subject of much debate.

Some scholars have questioned whether her oracle from YHWH commanding Barak to muster the troops warrants her designation

---

31. Amy Cottrill, "Joshua," 71.

32. Nira Yuval-Davis, *Gender & Nation*, Politics and Culture: A Theory, Culture & Society Series (London: Sage, 1997), 1.

as a prophet, since the oracle lacks the introductory deuteronomistic messenger formula, "Thus says YHWH." Instead, Deborah brings word from YHWH to Barak that he is to go up against the Canaanite general Sisera and YHWH will deliver him into Barak's hands. Furthermore, his response that he will go only if Deborah will accompany him and her consent have caused scholars to debate whether she should be regarded as a warrior. However, it is her reply—"I will surely go with you; nevertheless, the road on which you are going will not lead to your glory, for the Lord will sell Sisera into the hand of a woman" (Judg 4:6–9)—that has generated the greatest deliberation. The commentaries on Deborah's response have been broad ranging, from condemning Barak as a coward to accusing Deborah of usurping men's roles. The underlying theme in this debate is gender.

The caveat that the glory would go to a woman is taken as a rebuke of Barak for being unwilling to execute the masculine role of military hero. Given that violence is gendered masculine especially in the context of warfare, military service is a task that Barak is supposed to perform unquestioningly. By contrast, his hesitation is often understood as serving to "un-man" him by giving the impression that he is weak. Nevertheless, there is a fate worse for a man than being defeated by a woman in battle. It is being killed by a woman in battle. Although readers have been led to expect that Deborah would defeat Sisera, it is Jael, wife of Heber the Kenite, who brings about his demise. Sisera flees the battlefield on foot when his army comes under siege, and he is killed by Jael in her tent. Sisera's act of deserting the military theater and dying at the hands of a woman feminizes him, as demonstrated by the story of the final disposition of Abimelech, son of the judge Gideon. During an attack on a tower in Shechem, Abimelech is mortally wounded by a woman who drops an upper millstone on his head. Rather than risk people saying that he was killed by a woman, he asks his armor-bearer to finish him off (Judg 9:53–54). Harold Washington explains that the "male is by definition the subject of warfare's violence and the female its victim."[33] Therefore, in an ironic gender reversal, Gale Yee and others note that in these stories women often "become the means by which men are 'un-manned' or shamed."[34]

33. Harold Washington, "Violence and the Construction of Gender," *Biblical Interpretation* 5 (1997): 346.

34. Gale A. Yee, "By the Hand of a Woman: The Metaphor of the Woman-Warrior in Judges 4," *Semeia* 61 (1993): 115.

From a womanist perspective, Sisera's character has avoided being interpreted as the hypermasculinized black male rapist and Jael as the hypersexualized black female seductress in racialized and gendered stereotypes in US public discourse. In Sisera's case, it is likely because he is not a sexual threat to the purity of an Israelite woman. Jael escapes being racialized because, unlike Jezebel, she is considered a "good" foreign woman (see below). However, she does not avoid being sexualized, as she is often depicted as a seductress. Nevertheless, Sisera, in yet another reversal, is perhaps doubly othered by being killed by Jael. First, according to some scholars, he is othered by the manner in which Jael kills him. Some interpreters have sexualized her use of a tent peg to kill him as a phallic symbol, putting her in the male role of rapist and feminizing him.[35] But his foreignness also serves to un-man him, as foreign men in Judges are known to be feminized in order to discredit them. As Susanne Scholz observed regarding Moabite men, "They are feminized, sexualized, dehumanized, and hence discredited as foreigners, the others, who deserve contempt, ridicule, sexual violence, and even murder."[36]

Even when women are nowhere near the military combat, they are still the objects of male violence. Feminist scholars were the first to focus on female victims of violence, such as Jephthah's daughter in Judges 11, the unnamed wife of Samson in Judges 13, and the Levite's concubine in Judges 19. Jephthah was the son of a man of Gilead and a woman of questionable sexual repute, who built a reputation as a mighty warrior. He defends Israel from the Ammonite threat and makes a vow to sacrifice the one who comes forth from his house if YHWH gives him victory. The first to greet him when he returns home victorious is his only child, a daughter. He fulfills his vow and offers up his daughter.

A number of scholars condemn Jephthah for sacrificing his daughter, suggesting that his illegitimate birth left him ignorant of Israel's prohibitions against human sacrifice. However, YHWH's silence in the matter suggests that Israel's deity does not condemn the ritual. It could be said, however, that Dtr ascribes Jephthah's downfall,

35. See, for example, Yee, "By the Hand of a Woman"; for a revised, more ambiguous evaluation of Jael's gender, see Gale A. Yee, "The Woman Warrior Revisited: Jael, Fa Mulan, and American Orientalism," in *Joshua and Judges*, ed. Athalya Brenner and Gale A. Yee, Texts @ Contexts series (Minneapolis: Fortress Press, 2013), 175–90.

36. Susanne Scholz, "Judges," in *Women's Bible Commentary*, ed. Carol A. Newsom, Sharon H. Ringe, and Jacqueline E. Lapsley, 3rd ed., 20th anniversary edition (Louisville: Westminster John Knox, 2012), 117.

and to a larger extent Israel's downfall, to his parentage. Lillian Klein contends that Dtr blames the actions of men like Abimelech and Jephthah on their fathers' illicit sexual relations: "Whether with foreign women (Gideon's concubine) or not (the harlot-mother of Jephthah), non-familial Israelite proliferation is shown as potentially destructive."[37]

Despite being born of ideal Israelite parentage, Samson's predilections for Philistine women lead Israel down a path to destruction. Susanne Scholz describes the Samson cycle as one where "patterns of masculinity and ethnocentrism intertwine."[38] Wil Gafney, in her womanist reading of Samson, writes that his story is one of "twisted games, riddles, and blood sport" that are "lethal" to the women in his life.[39] YHWH raises up Samson to deliver Israel from the subjugation of the Philistines. The Philistines, especially the women who have the misfortune to come into contact with him, are subjected to indiscriminate violence and threats of violence initiated by Israel's deity. Samson marries a Philistine woman over his parents' objections, but the narrator reports that the marriage was orchestrated by YHWH as a pretext for initiating hostilities with the Philistines (Judg 14:4). The writer portrays the Philistines as a major ethnic and military threat to the Israelites, perhaps because they represent a group of outsiders who literally invaded Canaan from without. Therefore, intermarrying with them is considered particularly egregious.

Although mothers may occasionally have a say in their son's choice for a marital partner (cf. Gen 21:21; 26:34–35), the giving and taking of women as wives is conducted between men. Therefore, Samson's Philistine wife becomes a bargaining chip between him and the men in her family. As such, she is readily dispensable. First, when the coordinated conflict ensues and she is situated between Samson and the Philistine men, her father takes her from Samson and gives her to his best man. When Samson demands her back, her father offers him her younger sister instead. Next, Samson declines the offer and strikes back at the Philistines by destroying their agricultural means for economic production. Finally, they in turn retaliate by killing Samson's wife and father. Ironically, this episode reveals how

37. Lillian Klein, *Triumph of Irony in the Book of Judges*, JSOTSup 68 (Sheffield: Almond, 1988), 99.

38. Susanne Scholz, "Judges," 121.

39. Wil Gafney, "A Womanist Midrash of Delilah," in *Womanist Interpretations of the Bible: Expanding the Discourse*, ed. Gay L. Byron and Vanessa Lovelace (Atlanta: Semeia, 2016), 51.

really bad things had gotten in Israel. Instead of Israel crying out for deliverance, they not only surrender to their domination by the Philistines but also cooperate in subduing Samson (Judg 15:9–13). Samson responds by killing a thousand Philistine men.

Yet, this is not the end of Samson's aggression toward the Philistines. Once more, a woman figures in the violence between Samson and the Philistines. Following a visit with a Philistine prostitute in Gaza, Samson meets and falls in love with a woman named Delilah (Judg 16:4). Delilah is an ethnically ambiguous character who might be an Israelite on her father's side, thereby placing her in a liminal state in the "us" versus "them" category. The Philistines use Delilah to capture Samson. Delilah is an independent woman who is not under the control of a father or husband. Nor is she a sex worker despite numerous attempts at defining her as a "quintessential femme fatale, the woman bringing down a successful man with her seductive irresistibility."[40] Interestingly, they are willing to pay her instead of using coercion for her compliance, although the readers are not told what would have happened if she had refused. Gafney describes Delilah as a woman who thankfully only suffers violence at the hands of her interpreters and not the writer. Yet, she also notes that neither Samson's wife nor Delilah is asked for her cooperation.[41]

In what could be interpreted as an act of self-preservation or the defense of her people, Delilah learns the secret of Samson's strength and reports it to the Philistine lords. They capture, bind, and torture Samson. In his final act of might, he prays to YHWH for the strength to avenge the Philistines. His hair has grown back, allowing him to regain his power. He uses his strength to bring down the roof of the temple, where the Philistines had brought him out to entertain them like Sarah Baartman of the "Hottentot Venus" notoriety (Judg 16:25).[42] The sexual connotation of Samson's "performance" before women and men, where he was likely stripped bare, would have been sexually humiliating.[43] Samson pushes against the pillars holding up

40. Scholz, "Judges," 121.

41. Gafney, "A Womanist Midrash of Delilah," 65–66.

42. Sarah Baartman (also Saartjie Baartman) was an eighteenth-century black South African woman brought to London for her exceedingly protuberant buttocks and displayed in "freak shows" across London and Paris.

43. Amy Kalmanofsky has pointed out that the Hebrew verb *sahaq/tsahaq* translated "to play" ("to entertain" in the NRSV) in Judg 16:25, 27, also means "to fondle a woman" in Gen 26:8. *Gender-Play in the Hebrew Bible: The Ways the Bible Challenges Its Gender Norms* (New York: Routledge, 2017), 88.

the roof, killing himself and more Philistine men and women in this one act than over his lifetime. The narrator reports that he judged Israel for twenty years.

GIRLY MEN AND DISFIGURED WOMEN

In what might be described as pro-monarchic propaganda, the downward spiral of the state of affairs in Israel portrayed by Dtr has reached its nadir with a series of events that are framed by the notice, "In those days there was no king in Israel; all the people did what was right in their own eyes" (Judg 17:4; 18:1; 19:1; 21:21). There is no defense of a national identity based on land, obedience to YHWH, or keeping a distance from the Canaanites. Most significantly, there are no more deliverers; there are no judges. The external threat to Israel's identity that Dtr warned about has evolved into an internal one, where Israelite men emasculate other Israelite men and Israelite women are fodder for men's power games.

Among the conduct that Dtr condemns as "right in the eyes of the people" was the establishment of an unauthorized cultic site in Israel, filling it with stolen objects and unsanctioned clergy, marauding, raiding, and plundering a defenseless city and a civil war. This could be interpreted as one among a number of acts that function to un-man the men of Israel. Ovidiu Creangă explains that a cornerstone of Dtr's representation of Joshua's masculinity is his ability to persuade the people to keep the Law.[44] Lawlessness is a signature of the final four chapters of the book of Judges, and the heinous acts committed serve to un-man most of the remaining men. The incident of Micah (Judg 17:1–6), who steals money from his mother and then sets up a shrine with an idol made of cast metal from the proceeds, acquires an ephod and teraphim and installs first his son and then a Levite as his priests, sets the cycle in motion.

The Danites are on their way to overtake the city of Laish when they stop by Micah's house and steal his idol, cultic objects, and priest to establish their own shrine at Laish, renamed Dan after the tribe's eponymous ancestor. Despite his protestations, "when Micah saw that they were too strong for him, he turned and went back to his home" (Judg 18:26). Like the men at Ai, Micah is un-manned by the fact that "to flee from before the enemy, i.e. to turn one's back and

---

44. Creangă, "Variations on the Theme of Masculinity," 97.

move inward, 'discredits' in masculine contests of war."[45] The writer
continues to recount the ongoing crimes committed in Israel in the
absence of a king. From the gang rape, murder, and dismemberment
of a certain Levite's concubine or wife of secondary rank—a story
that has earned the status of "text of terror"—to the slaughter of the
tribe of Benjamin and the subsequent kidnap and rape of the virgins
in Jabesh-Gilead and Shiloh to repopulate the Benjaminites, issues of
gender, sexuality, and class become entangled in a web of misogyny,
deceit, male honor, and genocide.

The Levite is forced to defend his honor at the threat of being
feminized sexually by the men of Gibeah, a reversal of the dishonor
shown him by his concubine when she left him for her father's home
(Judges 19). In raping his woman, the men of Gibeah still manage
to indirectly assert their power over the Levite. Ken Stone explains
that "although the men of Gibeah did not bring dishonor upon the
Levite directly by raping him *as if he were a woman*, they nevertheless
manage to challenge his honor in another way: *through his woman*."[46]
He lies to the other tribes about what took place, which leads to
the intertribal conflict and near annihilation of the Benjaminites, the
devotion to destruction of the men and women of Jabesh-Gilead
(except for four hundred virgins), and the abduction of another two
hundred virgins at Shiloh (Judges 20–21). Alice Keefe observes that
"there is an element of dark absurdity in both the horror of the
woman's fate at the hands of the Levite and the horror of a war
among the tribes which is to no purpose except mass death and more
rape."[47] The episode concludes with a report that the tribes returned
to business as usual, and the narrator repeats for the last time the
ideological exhortation that, "In those days there was no king in
Israel; all the people did what was right in their own eyes."

1 AND 2 SAMUEL: SEX, LIES, AND KINGSHIP

The books of 1 and 2 Samuel are accounts of the shift from a
decentralized form of tribal leadership in Israel to the centralization of
government under the monarchy first ruled by Saul and then David.
Although Dtr's pro-monarchic agenda is explicit in Judges 19–21,

45. Creangă, "Silenced Songs of Victory," 118.
46. Ken Stone, "Gender and Homosexuality in Judges 19: Subject-Honor, Object-Shame?"
JSOT 66 (1995): 100 (emphasis original).
47. Alice Keefe, "Rapes of Women/Wars of Men," *Semeia* 61 (1993): 92.

certain motifs in Joshua also suggests this sentiment. L. Daniel Hawk refers to a "centralizing agenda" in Joshua the way Israel is portrayed as one nation under YHWH. He remarks that, "Joshua repeatedly and emphatically renders Israel as one people (e.g., 'the whole nation,' 'all Israel,' the 'entire people')."[48] Despite the notice at the end of the book of Judges that Israel as a nation has devolved into a state of anarchy because there is no king, the narratives seem to be conflicted about the benefit of the monarchy in Israel.

Carol Meyers has argued that, in contrast to women in the tribal period, the development of the monarchy in Israel contributed to a decline in the status of women's leadership roles. Meyers contends that women experienced greater gender equality with men prior to the monarchy because "the decentralized and difficult village life of premonarchic Israel provided a context for gender mutuality and interdependence, and of concomitant female power."[49] However, similar to certain female characters who flex their muscle in *Game of Thrones*, the successful television show about the struggles between two royal families in a mythical medieval kingdom, a number of women in 1 and 2 Samuel demonstrate their power and influence. There are royal women, cunning women, wise women, and women who communicate with the dead to name a few.

First Samuel opens with the so-called rivalry-between-women motif (cf. Gen 16, 21; 30:1–22). Hannah, the mother of Samuel, the last judge in Israel and arguably the first prophet,[50] was barren until YHWH heard her cries and she conceived and gave birth to Samuel. Before Samuel's birth, Hannah has to contend with her husband's secondary wife Peninnah, who has children. Esther Fuchs notes the combination of the rivalry-between-women motif and the motherhood motif in this story as the "fertile Peninnah taunts and humiliates Hannah for her barrenness (1 Sam 1:16)."[51]

---

48. L. Daniel Hawk, "The Truth About Conquest: Joshua as History, Narrative, and Scripture," *INT* 66, no. 2 (2012): 135.

49. Carol Meyers, *Discovering Eve: Ancient Israelite Women in Context* (New York: Oxford University Press, 1988), 187; see also Jo Ann Hackett, "In the Days of Jael: Reclaiming the History of Women in Ancient Israel," in *Immaculate and Powerful: The Female in Sacred Image and Social Reality*, ed. Clarissa W. Atkinson, Constance H. Buchanan, and Margaret R. Miles (Boston: Beacon, 1985), 1–14.

50. Some scholars argue that Samuel should be considered the first prophet in Israel based on 1 Samuel 9:9. When Saul seeks the prophet Samuel, there is a parenthetical notice that formerly people in Israel sought a seer to inquire of YHWH.

51. Esther Fuchs, "The Literary Characterization of Mothers and Sexual Politics in the Hebrew Bible," in *Women in the Hebrew Bible: A Reader*, ed. Alice Bach (New York: Routledge, 1999), 136.

Samuel plays a significant role in the rise and fall of Saul. The elders in Israel requested of Samuel a king to govern them "like other nations" (1 Sam 8:5) and Saul is chosen from among the people (1 Sam 10:17–27; cf. 11:14). However, Samuel is a source of continued opposition to Saul's reign (1 Samuel 13–15). Even in death he torments Saul. When Saul seeks a word from YHWH for an impending Philistine incursion, all legitimate means of consulting YHWH are closed off, so he turns to necromancy, an unauthorized form of divination that he had banned in the land. He disguises himself and visits a woman necromancer (1 Sam 28:8–14). She fears for her life if she fulfills his request. Nonetheless, she brings up the spirit of Samuel from among the dead, who proceeds to rebuke Saul and pronounce the end of his reign (Judg 28:15–19). The necromancer is not condemned by Dtr here. Esther Hamori comments that, notwithstanding interpreters who have portrayed the woman at Endor as a foreigner, idolater, and "lady of the night," there is no "indication in the text that she is anything other than a Yahwistic diviner providing her services of religious access to the king."[52] First Samuel ends with Saul's death in battle against the Philistines (1 Samuel 31).

The deuteronomistic writer portrays David, Saul's successor, as a man sought by YHWH "after his own heart" (1 Sam 13:14). However, a closer look reveals an opportunist who, for example, agrees to become Saul's son-in-law for the prestige. First, he accepts Saul's daughter Merab for a wife, but then loses her to another man (1 Sam 18:17–19). Saul offers her sister Michal in her stead, hoping that David will be killed while trying to acquire the foreskins of a hundred Philistines for a bride price. Michal, however, loves David and helps him escape her father's attempt to kill him (1 Sam 19:11–17). Unfortunately, marriage to Michal is just a means to an end for David, who continues his campaign to undo Saul's kingship by withholding children from Michal (2 Sam 6:23).

David's marriage to his second wife, Abigail, provides him with a degree of financial security. The writer describes her as a wealthy woman with beauty and brains. Although there is no physical description of her, she demonstrates her wisdom by preventing David and his men from killing her husband, who lives up to his name

---

52. Esther Hamori, *Women's Divination in Biblical Literature: Prophecy, Necromancy, and Other Arts of Knowledge*, Anchor Yale Bible Reference Library (New Haven: Yale University Press, 2015), 113–14.

Nabal, "fool," by providing for them liberally of her husband's bounty (1 Sam 25:1–31). When her husband learns what she has done, he is paralyzed with fear and dies, freeing her to marry David. Shortly thereafter, he also takes Ahinoam as a wife (1 Sam 25:43). David will go on to take more wives, but none of his marriages is more controversial than his marriage to Bathsheba.[53] She too is another man's wife, but David commits adultery with her and impregnates her (2 Sam 11:2–5). David has her husband killed to cover up his crime and then makes her his wife. The child dies, but she conceives again and gives birth to Solomon (2 Sam 12:24).

David's offspring from multiple marriages contribute to dysfunctional family dynamics that bring him disappointment. When his firstborn son, Amnon, rapes his sister Tamar, David responds halfheartedly (2 Sam 13:1–22). Amnon's violation brings shame upon Tamar, reducing her to spend the rest of her days as a "desolate woman" in the house of her brother Absalom (2 Sam 13:20). In turn, her brother Absalom kills Amnon, then attempts to usurp the throne through engaging in sexual acts with David's concubines in the sight of "all Israel" (2 Sam 16:20–22). Jo Ann Hackett describes the motive as an effort to show that Absalom has "upstaged David in his masculine prowess, which is a major qualification for king."[54] Absalom is killed in battle and David mourns his death.

Before 2 Samuel comes to a close is a story explaining the final disposition of the house of Saul. In his zeal for the people of Israel and Judah, Saul attempts to annihilate the Gibeonites. Saul's bloodguilt causes a famine in the land that can only be terminated if David avenges the Gibeonites. David gives the sons of Saul's secondary wife Rizpah and his daughter Merab to the Gibeonites, who impale them and leave their corpses to rot as recompense for Saul's injustice (2 Sam 21:1–14). Rizpah is triply marginalized as a woman, wife of secondary status, and widow. Moreover, her sons are the innocent victims of state-sanctioned retributive justice. Yet, she protects the bodies of her and Merab's sons from desecration by the animals and elements, showing that she is more righteous than David. Stephanie Buckhanon Crowder expresses the anguish felt by the numbers of modern black mothers whose sons have been killed. She writes that, "Rizpahs today face death. It is not because they and their children are fodder in kingdom games. African American mothers walking in

---

53. For a list of David's wives, see 2 Sam 3:2–5 (cf. 5:13–16).
54. Hackett, "1 and 2 Samuel," 161.

the shoes of Rizpah today must guard children caught in the crossfire of unjust laws, vigilante neighbors, gangs, and unequal school discipline."[55]

1 AND 2 KINGS: RETURN TO THE WILDERNESS

First Kings is the climax of the deuteronomistic narrative and everything goes downhill from there. The kingdom of Judah comes to an end and the people are exiled to Babylon at the end of 2 Kings. First Kings begins with the final days of David's reign, which marks a new era in Israel's history. The narrator informs the reader of David's end by reporting that his virility has faded, a sign of his inability to effectively rule any longer. As evidence, the writer notes the absence of any sexual relations between David and Abishag, a beautiful Shunammite virgin that his servants brought in to keep him warm (1 Kgs 1:1–3).

THE CLASS/GENDER DIVIDE

Before the enfeebled David dies, he is manipulated into proclaiming Solomon the heir to the throne (1 Kgs 1:11–13) through what might be described as palace intrigue by the prophet Nathan and Bathsheba. As queen mother, Bathsheba carries influence over her son the king. Adonijah, the rightful heir to the throne, sentences himself to death when he asks Bathsheba to request that Solomon give him David's concubine Abishag for a wife. His request, to a lesser degree, is similar to Absalom's ploy to usurp the throne from David, but with the same effect. Solomon has him killed, and this is the last time we hear from Bathsheba (1 Kgs 2:13–24). Following Adonijah's death and the reorganization of the palace, Solomon is firmly established on the throne.

A superficial reading of the reign of Solomon offers the portrait of a mythological golden age of a united kingdom at peace with its neighbors and governed by a wise and wealthy ruler. However, a more realistic depiction is of a man who ascends the throne by deception, eliminates his nearest competition, enters into marriage alliances with foreigners, and accomplishes his building projects by

55. Stephanie Buckhanon Crowder, *When Momma Speaks: The Bible and Motherhood from a Womanist Perspective* (Louisville: Westminster John Knox, 2016), 60.

what we might today describe as class warfare. The ability of one group to appropriate the surplus labor product of another group creates unequal social classes.[56] In 1 and 2 Kings, these groups are separated into the tribute-imposing and the tribute-bearing classes; the former include royalty and other political elites and the latter consist of peasants, pastoralists, artisans, and slaves.[57] Solomon exacerbated these differences by redistricting the territory for tax collection purposes and imposing forced labor, or corvée, on both the Canaanites and the people of Israel (1 Kgs 5:13–17; 9:20–22).

The class divide is made more visible when gender and sexuality are inserted in the narratives, especially in the stories of sex workers and widows. Solomon's reputed wisdom is built on the judgment that he rendered between two sex workers in the same living quarters who give birth days apart. One woman lies on her son and kills him. She exchanges her dead son for the other woman's child while they slept. When the mother of the living son realizes the switch, she confronts the other woman, who denies that the dead child is hers. The two women take their dispute before Solomon, who offers to cut the living baby in half. The mother of the dead child accepts this solution. However, the mother of the living child protests and offers to give up the child rather than have him killed. Solomon discerns that the woman who shows the child compassion is his true mother (1 Kgs 3:16–28).

Although the story is intended to display Solomon's wisdom, it also highlights the vulnerability of women who live outside the patriarchal household, despite prostitution being tolerated in ancient Israel. The likelihood that they resided on the outskirts of town is an indication of their marginal status.[58] Moreover, their need to earn an income suggests that their pregnancies were only a minor inconvenience that interrupted, but did not stop, their work. Given their circumstances, giving birth to a son may have provided the women with an insurance policy for their future. In defense of the dead child's mother, Ken Stone offers that, "The deceptive prostitute can be understood as acting out of desperation rather than greed, for her survival may depend upon the son she has lost. At the same time, the compassion of the living child's mother is further underscored; for

56. Norman K. Gottwald, "Social Class as an Analytic and Hermeneutical Category in Biblical Studies," *Journal of Biblical Literature* 112, no. 1 (Spring 1993): 4.

57. Gottwald, "Social Class," 5–6.

58. As an example, Judah's daughter-in-law Tamar stationed herself at the entrance to Enaim, by the wayside, where he solicited her for sex (Gen 38:14, 21).

she is willing to give up the son who could provide for her in the future in order to ensure his own survival."[59]

The story of the widow rescued by the prophet Elisha also exposes the economic helplessness of women without benefit of a father or husband (2 Kgs 4:1–7). Her deceased husband was a member of Elisha's company of prophets. Threatening her future economic security, creditors want to take her two children as payment for her husband's debts. Elisha instructs the widow to fill as many vessels as she can with the little oil left in her home until it ran out, sell the oil to settle her debts, and live off the proceeds that were left. Although this story belongs to a series of miracle stories (cf. 2 Kgs 4:38–41, 42–44), it also sheds more light on the exploiters and the exploited.

BINARY REPRESENTATIONS OF FOREIGN WOMEN

Clearly, Solomon's burdensome economic policies were a causal factor for the division of the united kingdom. Referring to the corvée, Gottwald explains, "This onerous form of surplus extraction, coupled with taxation in kind had become a widespread class grievance on which the united monarchy foundered and then split when the Judahite ruling class failed to modify the policy."[60] Nevertheless, Dtr dresses the division in theological clothing fashioned as exogamy. The deuteronomistic writer blames foreign women for leading Israel to commit religious apostasy, beginning with Solomon's marriages to foreign women (1 Kings 11). In addition to being married to a daughter of an Egyptian pharaoh, he had an additional seven hundred foreign wives and three hundred concubines, whom Dtr contends influenced him to follow after other gods. As a consequence, YHWH promises to tear the kingdom from him, leaving him with one tribe for David's sake. For Dtr, a direct line is drawn from exogamy to apostasy. As David Janzen notes, a unifying theme in the DH is that "intermarriage with Canaanites causes the worship of other gods, which results in exile."[61]

For Dtr, foreign women represent otherness, something alien, seductive, and dangerous. Nevertheless, despite bearing the brunt of

---

59. Ken Stone, "1 and 2 Kings," in *The Queer Bible Commentary*, ed. Deryn Guest, Robert E. Goss, Mona West, and Thomas Bohache (London: SCM, 2006), 228.

60. Gottwald, "Social Class," 11.

61. David Janzen, *The Violent Gift: Trauma's Subversion of the Deuteronomistic History's Narrative*, Library of Hebrew Bible/Old Testament Series 561 (New York: T&T Clark, 2012), 22–23.

Dtr's condemnation for the demise of Israel, not all foreign women are considered wicked. Rather, foreign women in the DH are portrayed in binary opposites as good and bad. According to Nancy Nam Hoon Tan, foreign women are considered virtuous inasmuch as "(1) they are not seeking marriage with any Israelite men; (2) they are not portrayed as involved with any foreign religion; (3) they make confessions of the greatness and sovereignty of Yahweh."[62] Rahab is rewarded for extolling YHWH's might and Jael is blessed for cooperating with YHWH's military campaign. The Queen of Sheba is constructed as a "good Yahwist" for her speech praising Solomon for his good fortune: "Blessed be the Lord your God, who has delighted in you and set you on the throne of Israel!" (1 Kgs 10:9).[63] Likewise, the widow of Zarephath, who feeds and shelters the prophet Elijah during a famine despite the food insecurity she and her young son experience, proclaims that Elijah is a true prophet of a powerful deity when he resurrects her son who unexpectedly dies: "Now I know that you are a man of God and that the word of the Lord in your mouth is truth" (1 Kgs 17:8–24). Not only are none of these women shown worshiping their deities, but the Queen of Sheba departs without becoming another of Solomon's many wives.

On the flip side is the Phoenician princess Jezebel, the archetypal foreign woman who is guilty on all counts: she marries Ahab, king of Israel and she promotes the worship of the foreign deities Baal and Asherah while oppressing the prophets of YHWH. She has been called "wicked" for leading her husband, and by extension Israel, to do evil by worshiping other gods besides YHWH (1 Kgs 16:1–16), described as whoring and fornicating (2 Kgs 9:22). An unrepentant Jezebel is thrown to her death from a tower window, trampled underfoot by horses, and her remains eaten by dogs (2 Kgs 9:30–34). Tina Pippin explains, "The complex and ambiguous character of Jezebel in the Bible serves as the archetypal bitch-witch-queen in misogynist representations of women."[64] Yet, her reputation extends beyond the biblical text. A controlling image of black women since the antebellum period is the sexually aggressive "jezebels," created

---

62. Nancy Nam Hoon Tan, *The 'Foreignness' of the Foreign Woman in Proverbs 1–9: A Study of the Origin and Development of a Biblical Motif* (New York: De Gruyter, 2008), 174.

63. Walter Brueggemann, *1 & 2 Kings*, Smyth & Helwys Bible Commentary (Macon, GA: Smyth & Helwys, 2000), 134.

64. Tina Pippin, *Apocalyptic Bodies: The Biblical End of the World in Text and Image* (London: Routledge, 1999), 33.

by white slaveowners to justify their sexual exploitation of enslaved black women.

Athaliah, the daughter of Jezebel and Ahab, is the only woman monarch in Judah (2 Kgs 11:13–16). She comes to power when her son Ahaziah is killed and she murders the remaining heirs in the Davidic line, leaving her to assume the throne. Athaliah is not a foreigner, yet Dtr holds her responsible for spreading Baal worship in Judah, despite the lack of textual support for the association. She rules for seven years before the priest Jehoiada brings out of hiding a survivor of Athaliah's massacre and enthrones him in her place. Like her mother, she is violently put to death. Athaliah's guilt appears to have been the misfortune of being the offspring of intermarriage between an Israelite man and a foreign woman. As Tan contends, Dtr fears that the "foreign blood" running deep in Athaliah is enough of a threat to permanently contaminate the purity of Yahwism.[65] Athaliah's death brings the notorious Omride Dynasty to a close.

HULDAH: A DEUTERONOMISTIC PROPHET

The deuteronomistic writer depicts Josiah as the ideal ruler, unlike any other before him, "who turned to the Lord with all his heart, with all his soul, and with all his might, according to all the law of Moses" (2 Kgs 23:25). At the end of his reign, he institutes a number of religious reforms in response to the word of YHWH from the woman prophet named Huldah (2 Kgs 22:14–20). A copy of the book of the Torah is found in the temple and brought to the prophet Huldah for authentication. She consults YHWH and delivers an oracle of judgment on Judah for breaking the covenant with YHWH. In words that have been considered thoroughly deuteronomistic in their delivery, she prophesizes that YHWH would bring disaster on Judah and its inhabitants "because they have abandoned me and have made offerings to other gods, so that they have provoked me to anger with all the work of their hands, therefore my wrath will be kindled against this place, and it will not be quenched" (2 Kgs 22:17).

Although Josiah's reforms are largely regarded as evidence of his piety, feminist scholars are more suspicious of his motives. Judith McKinlay argues that the author uses Huldah's gender to eradicate

---

65. Tan, *The 'Foreignness' of the Foreign Woman*, 79.

the worship of Asherah in Judah, as part of the dismantlement of the high places, altars, and religious accouterments associated with the goddess. She writes that, "Huldah announces the words that give the warrant not only for the fall of Judah but for the fall of Asherah, the female figure of the divine for Israel."[66] Whatever accolades Dtr had for Josiah, he is killed in battle and Jerusalem falls to Babylon, bringing to a close 2 Kings and the end of the deuteronomistic narrative.

CONCLUSION

Important for the study of the DH is understanding that these are narratives about belonging and the politics of belonging. To belong is to be accepted as a member of a group, but the politics of belonging is about who gets to decide entry in the group. The writer establishes the criteria for who is a member of Israel in an exilic context that threatens the dissolution of that identity, defined primarily as covenant fidelity, possession of land, and avoidance of the ethnic other. Yet, the writer also engages in simultaneous and overlapping identity categories to establish and maintain the boundaries between the Israelite "us" and the foreign "them." Readers who bring feminist and intersectional perspectives to the deuteronomistic narratives are challenged with identifying where these multiple categories of identity intersect to discriminate against others. They must also confront the uncomfortable reality that the writer condones violence as part of Israel's identity formation, especially the relation between masculinity and masculine performance and violence against women, too often with the sanction of Israel's national deity or tacit approval by the deity's silence.

FOR FURTHER READING

Bachmann, Mercedes L. García. *Women at Work in the Deuteronomistic History*. International Voices in Biblical Studies 4. Atlanta: Society of Biblical Literature, 2014.

Crowell, Bradley L. "Good Girl, Bad Girl: Foreign Women in the Deuteronomistic History in Postcolonial Perspective." *Biblical Interpretation* 21, no. 1 (2013): 1–18.

66. Judith McKinlay, "Gazing at Huldah," *The Bible and Critical Theory* 1, no. 3 (2005): 4.

McKinlay, Judith E. *Reframing Her: Biblical Women in Postcolonial Focus*. Bible in the Modern World 1. Sheffield: Sheffield Phoenix, 2004.

Stone, Ken. *Sex, Honor, and Power in the Deuteronomistic History*. Sheffield: Sheffield Academic, 1996.

PART III

Prophecy

3.

The Challenge of Violence and Gender
under Colonization

CORRINE L. CARVALHO

INTRODUCTION

The prophetic books present a number of hurdles for contemporary readers of the Bible, especially those unfamiliar with the writing conventions of the ancient world. We have no modern parallel in the United States that functions in exactly the same way that prophets did in ancient Israel, so many new to the study of the prophets bring unhelpful assumptions to their reading of the material. For those who are studying for ministry, especially within traditions that use a lectionary, the challenge of preaching or teaching on the material can feel daunting.

The portrayal of gender diversity in the prophetic collections, as well as material that appears to our eyes as xenophobic, adds to the challenges of the material. Those studying for ministry need to process their own reactions to misogynistic and patriarchal elements in these books as part of their own spiritual and intellectual formation. While I will address contemporary audiences at the end of this essay, I proceed not with an eye to application but rather with the goal to aid the ministerial student's personal journey.

From an introductory feminist perspective, several features of these collections need to be addressed. These books are collections of highly rhetorical, literary texts, so contemporary readers immediately encounter their prominent rhetorical features. In this context, women function most prominently in metaphoric contexts. For example, Jerusalem is personified as a female both for good (Daughter Zion, who evokes empathy in Lamentations) and for ill (the adulterous wife of Hosea and Ezekiel). Although both metaphoric tropes stem from ancient Near Eastern literary conventions, they reinforce harmful gender stereotypes.

The history behind the text forms another important consideration for biblical interpretation, yet historical women are often invisible. Sometimes they are mentioned as collective groups, but the texts rarely invite the reader to see the material from the perspective of historical women. In addition, the biblical texts often address only one segment of the population: the elites, or those considered insiders from an Israelite perspective. This leaves invisible those who are marginalized: the "alien," the poor, the castrated, those who are sick, and so forth. These categories have an even greater impact on women, so it is important to address women's lives from the perspective of intersectionality.

The lives of those who represent other forms of gender diversity are even more invisible. As a result, readers often fill those spaces with modern assumptions about gender categories, roles, and orientations that did not apply to the ancient world. These assumptions are often accompanied by an unrecognized androcentrism (the assumption that "male" is the norm and, therefore, lacking unique gender elements) that has failed to examine ancient masculinities as social constructs as well. The impact on contemporary communities continues to be profound.

Finally, the prophetic books' ideal readers were quite distinct from contemporary real readers of these texts. Our theological concerns do not always match the concerns of these collections. As a result, this material, which was clearly theologically meaningful for its ancient audiences, is often experienced as theologically repugnant by contemporary audiences, especially around issues related to gender and difference. Can the original theological function of these texts be recovered, or can it only be rejected? While this essay will not answer that question, it will provide some strategies used by contemporary scholars.

WOMEN AS METAPHORS

Because biblical prophecy has no exact modern parallel, people new to this literature often come to it assuming that these texts were predictions of the future, and that their worth depended on their reliability as accurate predictors. The Near Eastern parallels found at Mari and Assyria, which seem to be primarily predictions, do not have the same level of literary artistry or variation as Israelite prophetic collections. While prophets did warn audiences about what might happen if a certain course of action continued, the primary goal in this body of literature was not prediction but rather persuasion.

The books of Amos, Hosea, and Isaiah contain a wide variety of literary forms, such as poetry, dirge, song, sermon, riddle, and so on, so any discussion of gender in these texts should be placed in the context of the literary conventions of the material. This means that the gendering of both people and concepts in the texts serves a larger literary purpose beyond historical representation. This caveat is immediately apparent in perhaps one of the first prophetic tropes to come under feminist scrutiny, the personification of cities as women.

The personification of cities as women has a robust literary history in Israelite prophetic literature. In some cases, the author uses the metaphor to portray the city as an innocent victim of violence. Jeremiah 31:15, for example, personifies Jerusalem as Rachel, one of the matriarchal founders of the tribes of Benjamin, Manasseh, and Ephraim (the latter two, sons of Joseph). Prophetic texts also employ the figure of "daughter Zion" when trying to evoke empathy for the city's fate as well as in texts promising restoration; this is perhaps most poignantly seen in the book of Lamentations (it occurs twenty-three times in the Hebrew Bible, eight of which are in Lamentations). Although Lamentations is not strictly prophecy but a collection of five poems mourning the fall of Jerusalem, the language used by the author so closely mirrors that of Jeremiah and other prophetic texts that it was traditionally understood as having been written by the historical Jeremiah. While not all of the references to daughter Zion are positive, she is not accused of sexual transgression. Her personification often parallels the actions of the goddess Ishtar in the Mesopotamian laments over the destruction of various cities. In both the Mesopotamian laments and many of the biblical texts, the female figure begs for the safety of the citizens of the city and weeps over their demise. For Judeans, the actions of daughter Zion replicate the activity of official female mourners referenced in Jeremiah 9:17. Although these tropes reinforce the gender stereotypes of the ancient world, as Maier points out they have garnered less contemporary focus within traditional analyses of Zion theology even though the gendered metaphor eventually becomes a "religious symbol of salvation."[1]

This is not the case for the other prominent trope of the city as a promiscuous woman and adulterous wife. The metaphor is applied to both enemy cities, such as the Assyrian city of Nineveh in the book of Nahum, and to Israelite cities, most often Jerusalem. When describing a foreign city, the female is not designated as God's wife. In Nahum 3:4, the personified city is a prostitute (or promiscuous) and an enchantress whom God shames (vv. 5–6) and then punishes (v. 10). The Israelite prophets personify the city as God's promiscuous wife in order to engage covenant language, depicting the Israelite city as the one who has broken the covenant. The physical punishment meted out by God as a consequence also derives from the realities of Israelite marriage, where a wife caught cheating can be both shamed and physically harmed by the cuckolded husband. While this trope occurs less often in the prophetic texts (primarily in Isaiah 57, Jeremiah 2–3, and Ezekiel 16 and 23 as well as Hosea 1–3), the way that the texts linger over the metaphor and the abhorrent pictures that they draw makes the impact of these metaphors extremely powerful. This figure is found in a number of prophetic texts, including Jeremiah and Ezekiel. I will focus on its use in Hosea.

In Hosea 1–3 the boundaries between history and metaphor are constantly blurred. On the one hand, the text, which seems to be a brief biography, projects Gomer as Hosea's historical wife. Yet the text is also explicit about the metaphorical function of the wife within the book. The author includes images of Gomer not for the sake of historical accuracy but to enhance the prophetic indictment of Israel's sins. The figure of an adulterous wife has been deliberately chosen to evoke disgust and revulsion. Personalizing her by attaching her to a beloved prophet enhances that evocative function.

In general, metaphors depend on the cultural or symbolic meaning given to a particular thing, but using an item or action as a symbol also reinforces the cultural meaning ascribed to that item. The

---

1. Christl M. Maier, *Daughter Zion, Mother Zion: Gender, Space, and the Sacred in Ancient Israel* (Minneapolis: Fortress Press, 2008), 4.

marriage metaphor, that is, the trope that Israel's worship of other gods is like a wife who cheats on her husband, in Hosea 1–3 depends on assumptions about women as sexual beings, legally subordinate to their husbands. Ezekiel's use of the metaphor enhances assumptions about women as uncontrollably lusty. Academic readers recognize that these metaphors do not aim to blame the fall of Jerusalem on the sexual violations of women; female sexual transgression is a metaphor for elite males' worship of other gods, or transgression of their covenant relationship with God. But the detail that the author provides in the metaphors, along with Hosea's rhetorical strategy to tie the metaphor to a real woman, easily reinforces negative views of women's sexuality.

Within its historical context, the metaphor reflects the status of women within the household, which itself springs from ancient views of human biology. The fact that women have eggs was not discovered until the seventeenth century CE, and the dual roles of sperm and egg were not confirmed until the late nineteenth century.[2] As a result, children were viewed as a man's property since they grew from the matter provided by the man, with the woman only providing heat and incubation. Inheritance and custody laws reflected the assumption that children were men's property. This meant that women's sexuality had to be controlled so that a man would know the paternity or ownership of any child. As a result, marriage was polygamous for men, but not for women.

Wives were also the legal property of their husbands. Once they were betrothed to a man, which could occur as early as infancy for rich families, females were legally bound to only have intercourse with their husbands. Adultery was a capital offense, punishable by stoning. Israelite law included a proviso that allowed a man who suspected a wife of adultery to bring her to trial at the temple. The ritual described in Numbers 5:11–31 includes the priest disheveling the hair of the accused wife, an act that shamed her. Men could also beat their wives; there is no mention of criminal domestic abuse in the Bible nor do the laws recognize rape within marriage, since a woman had no right to refuse intercourse with her husband (although purity laws did limit when intercourse should occur). These elements of husbands physically punishing and publicly

2. M. Cobb, "An Amazing 10 Years: The Discovery of Egg and Sperm in the 17th Century," *Reproduction in Domestic Animals* 47 (2012): DOI: 10.1111/j.1439-0531.2012.02105.x.

shaming adulterous wives lie behind texts such as Hosea 2:3 and 10, as well as Ezekiel 16:35–43.

Feminist biblical scholars have traced how these texts have supported elements of Christian culture harmful to women. The images reinforce cultural assumptions that continue to sexualize and objectivize women. This includes official stances, such as the failure to recognize rape within marriage or the lack of prohibition for many forms of domestic abuse, as well as informal cultural norms (e.g., women as primarily sexual beings, subordinate and more carnal than males) that have led to social failures to protect women from any form of rape or sexual assault. For example, the contemporary obsession with the dress and actions of young women who accuse men of rape replicates texts like Ezekiel 16:30–34 that portray the woman as the paying customer.

The metaphor of God as wronged husband also introduces the topic of gendered metaphors applied to God. Contemporary readers of the Bible often assume that language applied to God aims to exalt God and depict God as divinely perfect. The application of a metaphor of a male who shames and beats women does not jibe with this assumption. At the beginning of second-wave feminism (the feminist movement that arose in the 1970s), Mary Daly stated, "If God is male, then the male is God."[3] In other words, divinized masculine traits shape contemporary cultural assumptions of not only acceptable male behavior but what it means to be an honorable man. The prophetic marriage metaphor, consequently, continues to form and inform contemporary constructions of gender categories.

What is often missed is that this hypermasculine view of God is not the only gendered image applied to the divine body in the prophetic texts. Although rare, there are places where God is depicted as female. The most obvious passages are Isaiah 42:14 where God is likened to a woman in childbirth, and Hosea 11 where God nurtures baby Israel. To be sure, these positive images also reinforce gender stereotypes, where women's worth is tied to procreation and nurturing, but less often have these passages been used to flip Daly's warning into "If God is female, then the female is God."

So are there images of God as female that challenge gender assumptions in the prophets? Unfortunately, we bring our assumptions about gendered behavior to these texts, which makes

3. Mary Daly, *Beyond God the Father: Toward a Philosophy of Women's Liberation* (Boston: Beacon, 1972), 18.

identifying subversive metaphors difficult. For example, most readers of the Bible assume that divine warrior metaphors cast God as unswervingly male, but in the ancient Near East, such an assumption is erroneous. All of the polytheistic cultures surrounding Israel had warrior goddesses. In Ugarit, just north of Israel, the goddess Anat slays soldiers and laughs as she wades in blood and gore. In Mesopotamia, the most prominent goddess, Ishtar, fights on the battlefield with her servant kings. In Egypt, the goddess Sekhmet is so violent that the only way her violence could be stopped was by dying beer red so that, thinking it was blood, she drank it and passed out. This mythic language challenges modern assumptions that every warrior image in the Bible casts Yahweh as a male deity.

Isaiah 34:6 and 63:1 contain images of Yahweh as warrior slaughtering the people in Edom at the city of Bozrah. The details in these texts depict God as covered in gore, an image found in descriptions of both Anat and Sekhmet wading in blood. Sekhmet is associated with the lion, as is Yahweh as destroyer in passages such as Isaiah 31:4, Jeremiah 49:19, and Hosea 13:7–8. Anat, on the other hand, is accompanied by predatory birds. God's battle against Magog results in a gory feast for the birds in Ezekiel 39:17–20, while in Jeremiah 49:22 God becomes a predatory bird, an eagle swooping down on the enemy, making them "like the heart of a woman in labor." These representative examples demonstrate that readers should be cautious about applying contemporary definitions of gender directly onto ancient texts.

THE HIDDEN LIVES OF REAL WOMEN

As is true for many biblical books, the lives of real women are often invisible in the prophetic texts. Very few historical women appear, even fewer actually named. Occasionally passages reflect some specialized social groups of women, but these texts assume that the reader knows what these groups did and how they functioned within Israelite society. Feminist scholarship has tried to raise up these invisible women, both by bringing forward references to unnamed groups and individuals, as well as noting where women's presence must be assumed. This work has provided biblical scholarship a fuller view of the ancient world lying behind the texts.

Outside of the metaphoric use of Rachel mentioned above, only a few historical women are mentioned in the prophetic texts. Micah

6:4 includes Miriam with her brothers, Moses and Aaron, as leaders of the Exodus; this is the only reference to a woman known outside of the prophetic collection. Three prophetic texts refer to women who are sexual partners of the prophets: Isaiah 8:1–4; Hosea 1:1–3; and Ezekiel 24:15–27. Each of the passages is recounted to serve as a metaphor for military devastation, two of which refer to the destruction of cities, and each passage offers its own interpretive challenge. The most straightforward passage is the one in Ezekiel, which recounts the death of his wife, but then proceeds to liken her death to the fall of the temple in Jerusalem. This text explicitly says that Ezekiel himself is a "sign" (vv. 24 and 27), meaning that even the persona of the prophet has a metaphoric function. Scholars have had even more debate about whether Hosea's marriage to Gomer should be read literally or as an allegory. Again, the text quite explicitly states that Hosea's marriage is a metaphor depicting the sinfulness of Israel. Lastly, the passage in Isaiah 8 does not call the woman who gives birth to Isaiah's children his wife, but rather a prophet. We do know that prophets performed actions meant to symbolize an oracular message, and so scholars debate whether this pericope should be read as another case of a wife serving a symbolic function or if it describes a symbolic act performed by two prophets. Notice, then, that in these instances where contemporary audiences hope to find historical women, the texts use women's sexual and procreative identities to symbolize historical events, mostly controlled by elite males.

The book of Jeremiah contains three references to the prophet's mother, although in each passage she is equated solely with her uterus. The first allusion occurs in the first chapter, in which God claims to have formed Jeremiah in "the" womb to be a prophet, a passage that seems to disassociate the uterus from the female body (1:5); Isaiah 49:1 makes a similar statement about the servant God sends to restore them. The other two passages come from Jeremiah's laments where the prophet bemoans his fate. In 15:10 he laments that his mother ever gave birth to him, while in 20:16–18 he wishes his mother's womb had been his grave. The impact of these last two texts assumes the deep cultural importance of procreation associated with female uteri.

Motherhood as a rhetorical device is perhaps nowhere more obvious than the famous passage in Isaiah 7:10–17 that refers to a young pregnant woman. The history-like narrative recounts an encounter between the prophet Isaiah and the king of Judah, Ahaz, during a time when Judah was being pressed to join an alliance of other nations in the Levant to oppose the Assyrian advance. Many of Isaiah's oracles warn against joining such an alliance. In this passage, the prophet tells Ahaz that in less than five to six years (when, according to ancient accounts, children developed moral reasoning), those who were threatening to attack Jerusalem would all be destroyed. The pregnant woman simply becomes a convenient way to symbolize time.

While the passage is straightforward enough, however, the name of the child in verse 14 spawned more debate about the identity of this woman. The Greek translation of the Old Testament, the Septuagint, translated the Hebrew word for "young woman" as "virgin." The author of Matthew 1:23 quotes the Greek version of Isaiah 8:14 as being fulfilled by the birth of Jesus, thus making the woman in Isaiah a symbol of the virgin Mary, and "Immanuel" (or "Emmanuel" in the New Testament NRSV) a title for Jesus. But this passage, which never identifies this woman or the father of the child, simply reflects the trope seen in both Isaiah and Hosea where the names of women's children extend the symbolic functions of the mothers. The fact that "God is with us" will be obvious when the nations Ahaz fears are destroyed and Jerusalem is safe once again.

Prophets refer to groups of women more often than they do individual women; these groups usually have an identifiable social role. Sometimes these texts contain glimpses into women's lives otherwise not preserved in biblical texts. One such passage is Ezekiel 13:17–23, which is part of a long chapter condemning all kinds of false prophets. These verses focus on groups of female prophets, a group rarely referenced in other biblical texts. To be sure, there are a few named female prophets in the Old Testament, such as Deborah and Huldah, but they appear to act as individuals, rather than part of what scholars call a prophetic guild. Outside of Israel, however, evidence for groups of female religious functionaries exists, so it is not surprising that there would be similar groups in Israel. This derogatory passage in Ezekiel describes some of the actions of this group of professional women, but the exact nature of these actions remains obscure. What is not ambiguous, however, is that the condemnation does not focus on their gender. The first sixteen verses condemn male prophets, not because they are male but because they are false. The same is true in these verses. Thus, Ezekiel 13 does reveal that there was at least one publicly recognized group of female prophets in Jerusalem at the end of the monarchy.

In a similar way, Jeremiah 9:17–22 describes the actions of a group of professional female mourners. Here the passage condemns the male elite; verse 23 connects their deaths with hubris. The author mentions the women, not in a derogatory fashion, but to establish a funerary scene. The passage assumes that the audience knows the function of this social group within the funerary rituals. Neither Ezekiel 13 nor Jeremiah 9 refers to the marital status, sexuality, or procreative functions of these women. Here then we find prophetic references to women outside of the more prominent spheres of sexuality and procreation.

A social group of women that is occasionally condemned is elite women. Amos 4:1–3 depicts this group as lazy, ordering their husbands to bring them some refreshment, thus reversing honorable gender roles. Amos calls these women "cows." Scholars debate whether this is a derogatory term as it is in contemporary speech (meaning that they are fat and lazy), or whether it had a positive function given the ways cows are used in Near Eastern iconography to depict fertility and abundance. If it is the latter case, then the passage starts by addressing them with an honorific title, making the reversal of the fortune in verses 2b–3 even more striking.

Isaiah 3:16–26 denounces another group of elite women. Here the focus is on their lavish dress. Archeological excavations have revealed that in the Assyrian period, in which this passage is set, there was a rise of luxury goods throughout the Levant, including Jerusalem. These goods came from a marked up-tick in international trade and would have included increased supplies of precious metals, perfumes, and fine fabrics. This passage uses these luxury items as symbols of the hubris of these women, and contrasts their exalted position symbolized by these items with the diseased and enslaved bodies that they would become after their city fell.

NOT ALL WOMEN ARE CREATED EQUAL

Throughout the Bible there are references to classes of those that did not enjoy elite status: the widow, the orphan, and the resident alien. The Hebrew words translated by these terms do not exactly correspond to their meaning within ancient Israelite society. "Widows" would mean any adult woman not attached to a landowning male, either as wife or sister of a landowner, or as someone who had been divorced by an elite male, or someone whose husband was missing, a fate that happened far more often in the ancient world than it does today. Prophetic texts also reflect the social fragility of this class of women as illustrated in the book of Ruth. Some of the passages condemn elites for the treatment of widows and other vulnerable groups (see, for example Isa 1:23; Jer 22:3; and Zech 7:10), while others, such as Isaiah 10:2 and Jeremiah 15:8, and 18:21, use the term to represent the death of males in war.

Not every landless person was poor, nor was every landowner rich. The prophets allude to the poor as a general class, but again the life of poverty impacted women more than men. Within a household, men would be fed first and would get the best food available, children would come second, and only then adult women. This meant that these women would tend to get the worst food, including that which was spoiled. The effects of starvation on pregnant and nursing women would take a far greater toll on their bodies than on males. Fathers viewed daughters as a fiscal liability, as is attested by the fact that a prospective bridegroom must pay the bride's father to compensate for the cost of raising her.

It is unrealistic to talk about poor women without also talking about the context of sex workers in the ancient world. Although we do not have the voices of these women, it is not difficult to imagine where they would have come from or what their life would have been like. The book of Ruth seems to assume that poor women were vulnerable to sexual aggression (cf. Ruth 2:9, 22). For women who were starving and who had either already been raped or knew the reality of imminent rape, having intercourse in exchange for money, food, or tradable goods would have seemed like a logical option. Prophetic texts such as Amos 7:17 and Joel 3:2–3 recognize the increase in sex work during times of communal crisis.

For many years, scholars assumed that Herodotus's portrayal of cultic prostitution in Babylon was accurate, and they garnered biblical texts to support that conclusion. Even though there is some evidence for some kind of sacred marriage ritual in Mesopotamia, there is no evidence that it existed in ancient Israel. The discussion does raise the question of what ritual roles women may have had. In both Egypt and Mesopotamia, female priests could attain high rank. In fact, at the time of the Babylonian exile, the priestess who had the title "the God's Wife" was the second most important person in

Egypt. There is little evidence of Israelite women having an official religious leadership role, except perhaps as prophets (although there is also a large debate on whether or not Israelite prophets were part of the official temple system).

When the prophetic books do mention women participating in religious rituals, they do so to condemn them. Perhaps the two clearest examples are the inclusion of the women weeping for Tammuz in Ezekiel 8:14–15 and the diatribe against women worshiping the Queen of Heaven in Jeremiah 44. The passage in Ezekiel is the second of three examples of ritual violations taking place in the temple of Jerusalem after the first exile of the elite in 597 BCE. It is bookended by the violations of male elders (Ezek 8:11) and twenty-five people (translated as "men," but it could also be a mixed-gender group; Ezek 8:16) with their backs toward the temple. While the nature of the rituals in verses 11 and 16 remains speculative, the weeping for Tammuz is known from Mesopotamian texts. Tammuz (also known as Dumuzi) was a human male lover of the goddess Ishtar (also known as Inanna). There are different versions of this myth, but they all portray Tammuz as a dying and rising figure associated with the changes in growing seasons. In other words, the text in Ezekiel associates sinful women with foreign fertility rituals that emphasize sexuality and fertility, including procreation.

The identity of the Queen of Heaven in Jeremiah 44 is less clear. Several goddesses had that title in both western Asia and Egypt. The first ten verses in the chapter denounce the religious practices of Judean refugees and immigrants. The passage focuses on the whole community's participation in rituals that the author associates with the dominant, foreign culture. The text reveals that the issue revolves around ethnic identity: if these displaced persons adapt so much to Egyptian culture that they even worship their gods, then Judah's remnant would cease to exist as a distinctive group. Verses 11–14 state that the threat of violent destruction hangs over the community. The passage as a whole reflects the fact that immigrant and refugee populations encounter a double-bind. If they do assimilate into the culture, as the community seems to do in verses 1–10, they may have greater safety and security, but Jeremiah 44:11–17 suggests that such an attempt would be in vain, and that, as the permanent Other within the Egyptian society, they will never escape the threat of ethnic-based violence.

Verses 15–19 switch the blame onto the active role taken by female refugees in this ritual observance. The passage says that they were the ones making the offerings, suggesting that they may have had an official, priestly role in these liturgies. The people respond defiantly to the call for them to give up their practice, connecting the ritual directly to respite from both war and famine. The passage's explicit mention of female ritual activity in verses 9, 15, and 19 suggests that the women sought protection from rape and starvation that impacted women more than men. The passage does its best to depict these women as wholly evil: brazen, idolatrous, and heretical; interestingly, they are not sexualized. Yet at the same time it reveals that historically women probably maintained worship of goddesses who seemed better attuned to the experiences and plight of women in such a patriarchal world.

Most of the passages that casually refer to women in the prophetic collections reflect the fate of women during mass colonization. The reference to ropes in Isaiah 3:24 alludes to the ropes used to transfer enslaved populations to new locations. Exile, forced migration, refugee status: all of these experiences differed for men and women. Most of the prophetic books are set during either the Assyrian, the Babylonian, or the Persian conquests. Each of these empire-builders had different strategies in dealing with the elite native populations that they conquered. Assyria scattered them throughout its empire, Babylon settled them in groups in Mesopotamia, while Persia preferred to leave people in their native lands as long as they did not threaten Persian ascendancy. Sometimes the prophetic references to exile note the presence of wives and daughters among the members of households. A few of the poems in the prophets, however, add references to sexual violations in order to evoke either disgust or empathy from the audience. Certainly Joel 3:2–3 provides one example of this rhetorical feature.

Women who survived a siege would often be raped by the conquerors. This demonstrated ownership by the conqueror over everything the other male possessed. Those who survived the war, and the subsequent rape, could be claimed as plunder by the triumphant warriors (Isa 10:2). As plunder, they fell into permanent slave status, and, as the slave laws in the Pentateuch make clear, they were sexually available for the men of the household. These realities are reflected most explicitly in Lamentations 5, which outlines the various ways families were destroyed at the end of a siege: rape, torture, hard labor, to name a few. One of the main purposes of sexual violence was shaming of the male elite, who must face the reality that they could not protect the women within their household.

Even positive portrayals of women in the prophets primarily address male experience of exile. The portrayal of Ezekiel's wife as someone who was his "delight" (24:16), which presents a positive portrayal of a woman, compares the destruction of the temple of Jerusalem to the death of Ezekiel's wife, who remains unnamed. The parallel depends on the characterization of her as pleasing to and treasured by her husband. The grief he feels at her death becomes the measuring stick for the exiles' grief over the fall of the city. The point of the passage is God's command that they may not mourn these losses, a fate depicted as almost worse than the deaths themselves. This passage sharply demonstrates the focus on male experience.

In spite of the references to a few specific women, either as groups or individuals, the vast number of women addressed in the prophetic collections remain not just unnamed, but completely unmentioned. The threats of famine, disease, and violent death spelled out repeatedly in the prophetic texts were, in reality, meted out on women and girls, as much if not more than on the men and boys of Judah. For every king that a prophet denounced, there were a number of primary and secondary wives whose bodies would undoubtedly bear the brunt of the king's punishment. Women who invisibly served at the temple, weaving and doing other chores, would be among the slain. Destitute women who had become household slaves would be annihilated or reenslaved as part of a conquered landowner's household. While sex workers may have been among those most likely to survive, their ranks would have grown with an influx of displaced, impoverished, raped, and starving women, thus threatening the livelihood of such work. For the vast majority of the women who shared what these texts describe as God's wrath, the prophets remained silent.

FROM FEMINIST THEORY TO GENDER ANALYSIS

Women were not the only ones who experienced sexual violence in times of war. Many of the prophetic texts describe the men on the losing side of a battle as having been turned into women. Jeremiah 30:6 likens the pain of death on the battlefield to labor pangs. The condemnation of Babylon in Jeremiah 50–51 twice threatens that its warriors will become women (Jer 50:37 and 51:30). While this has often been taken as a metaphor for the shame felt by men who were weak and defeated, there may have also been a more literal meaning to these passages. At least some of the boys and men who were captured would have been castrated. Certainly, the iconography from both Egypt and Mesopotamia portrays eunuchs as regular parts of the monarchic retinue. In addition, it is not far-fetched to assume that some men were raped and sodomized by victorious soldiers. The law against sodomy in Leviticus 18:22 describes the act as turning a man into a woman, a notion echoed in the prophetic literature.

This use of the term "woman" assumes stable definitions of both male and female. Gender and queer studies have turned to broadening feminist focus on the lives of women to the analysis of all gender identity as a social construct. In societies that view gender as binary, meaning that there are only two gender categories (male and female), each of the categories tends to be defined in relation to the other. Men are strong, rule driven, and decisive, while women are soft, relational, and nurturing. One can see how quickly conceptual categories of masculinity and femininity become descriptions of concrete men and women. Many parts of the world today, including a large segment of the United States, share this binary view of gender. Many contemporary gender analyses of the Bible, however, would view gender as a fluid category, more a continuum than a system of opposites. For example, these gender analyses would recognize characteristics, such as nurturing or decisive, but would refrain from associating them with a particular gender. Gender scholars have also worked to distinguish between social gender identity, biological sexual assignment, and sexual orientation.

People have long assumed that ancient Israel had a strictly binary view of gender. While there are certainly biblical texts that do seem to assume dichotomous gender, the prophetic books have a number of passages that suggest a broader concept of gender identities. We have looked at a number of elements of traditional female identity above, but notice that these are based on social function and not on personal characteristics. The emphasis on women as sexual beings and agents of procreation reflects their function from the perspective of elite males. Even promiscuity and adultery are male problems in these texts, not female ones. To be sure, sex and procreation were hugely important in an Israelite woman's life, since her social status and economic security depended on having the right children (sons) with the right men (landowners). In a world where high infant mortality and childhood death led to a constant labor shortage, the whole community's well-being depended on the fertility of the women.

The biblical texts also reflect certain views about masculinities, depending on the social location of the man. Prophetic texts attest to a variety of male groups. Male heads of household and elders were supposed to impregnate the right women, protect the members of the household, and maintain a harmonious micro-community through their wise management. Warriors were expected to be strong, brave, and pious; priests were to be fair, knowledgeable, and focused on serving the deity. Scribes were educated civil servants, and kings should be wise, just, and humble. The prophetic texts often sound as if the whole population of Israel was sinful. They often offer sweeping condemnations of Israelite society, but every once in a while there is a glimpse into the reality that these texts are focused on the behaviors of elite, ruling males and the social codes that structured their behaviors.

The prophetic books often portray the prophet as clinging to the edges of social acceptability. This is due in part to the performative nature of prophecy itself. Most prophetic speech aims to change behavior, and therefore it uses rhetorical elements of persuasive speech, such as hyperbole and surprise or controversy. Prophetic books usually portray their eponymous prophets proclaiming in public, with or without other elements of performance. Certainly, the prophetic symbolic acts were performative. Yet these acts often included elements that distanced the prophet from acceptable masculine elite behavior. In Isaiah, the prophet walks around naked for three years to symbolize the threatened fate of the city's inhabitants (ch. 20). Ezekiel cooks his food on animal dung in chapter 3, while Jeremiah traverses the city with a yoke on his back (Jer 27:1–11). The gender performance of many male prophets explicitly plays with and sometimes subverts traditional masculine roles.

This distancing of the prophet from standard performances of masculinity is seen perhaps most clearly in the figure of Jeremiah. There are a number of ways that the book subverts his masculine identity. God forbids him from participating in the most expected elements of masculine performance: marrying and having children (16:1–9). He is not allowed to attend weddings and funerals which an honorable man would do, but he is instead identified with the female mourners. God "entices" or seduces him in 20:7, rendering him as female in relationship to God, and he inverts female fertility when he wishes his mother's womb had been his grave.

Jeremiah's portrayal makes more sense in the context of the broader ancient Near Eastern intersections of gender and religion. In Mesopotamia, the goddess Ishtar was often served by a class of priests who performed as having fluid gender. For example, although they had male names, the texts identify them as female. In certain religious processions, they dressed as half male and half female. Ishtar herself combined masculine traits (warrior) with feminine traits (fertility and sexuality). The book of Jeremiah often describes defeat in battle in similar gender terms. Warriors are compared to women giving birth in 30:6; the Babylonians are turned into women in 50:37 and 51:30; and the community is depicted as raped women in 13:20–27.

Ancient Israelite society did not connect sexual acts with gender identity in the same way as the modern world. Marriage and procreation did not depend on an emotional connection between husband and wife; it was a contractual relationship that provided a variety of benefits for society at large, including the smooth transferal of property rights from one generation to another. While there were instances of husbands and wives loving each other (and perhaps Ezekiel is one example of this), the marriage itself did not require this. The husband's duty was not to love but to procreate. As long as a man fulfilled this duty and protected the family, his physical relationships with other people who were legally available to him did not matter. In this light, Jeremiah's perennial bachelorhood was a greater social violation than if he had been married but also had a queer gender identity or same-sex sexual orientation.

This focus on procreation is seen in the reference to eunuchs in Isaiah 56:3–8. This material reflects the situation in Jerusalem after the rebuilding of the temple in the Persian period. The text discusses whether eunuchs and foreigners can offer sacrifices at the temple. While the passage in Isaiah is too late to reflect mutilation immediately following the fall of Jerusalem, men in royal service were also sometimes castrated, as is seen in royal iconography from both Mesopotamia and Egypt. According to Leviticus 21:20 a man with damaged testicles could not participate in sacrificial rituals, a condition met by those who had been castrated. Issues of Judean identity lie behind the discussion of eunuchs and foreigners in Isaiah 56. In Jeremiah 38:7–13 the prophet is saved by a eunuch serving in the court of Zedekiah. The passage provides his name, Ebed-Melech, which suggests his prominence, but the text also notes that he is a foreigner, placing both his foreignness and his gender identity within the broader context of colonization. The text in Isaiah 56 that deals with the same two social categories suggests that the community in control of the temple during the Persian period was wrestling with a purity prohibition that essentially ostracized men for being victims of colonization. Isaiah 56 explicitly reverses the ruling, first by rendering ritual memorials as a substitute for being childless (v. 5) and then by stating they can participate in sacrifices (v. 7). In this way, the text recognizes that these men were not childless because they refused to do their manly duty but because they had been mutilated so that they could not procreate.

Many biblical texts that refer to intercourse are concerned with the duties to procreate, rather than gender identity or sexual orientation. The fact that gender diversity among women has no reflex in the prophetic texts reinforces this conclusion, since sexual acts between women had no effect on procreation. When we reengage ancient assumptions about human biology discussed earlier, the practice of castration takes on an even more terrifying role. If ancient people assumed that children came from semen, then castration was a form of genocide. Castration not only shamed men, it cut off their name from the earth and annihilated families, clans, and potentially tribes. When coupled with postwar rape, the paired sexual violations literally attempted to root out the conquered nation.

GENDER AND RESTORATION

Since most prophetic texts reflect cultural memories of nationally traumatic events, it is not surprising that the bulk of their material centers on various forms of social collapse. This may surprise many Christian readers of these books, especially those from religious communities that use a lectionary, which often does not contain this dire material. For many Christians, the prophets are social innovators, champions of the poor, heralds of the Messiah, and saintly figures dedicated to God. This point of view is not totally incorrect. Many of these images come from parts of the books that imagine the creation of a perfect Israel in some indefinite future. Feminist biblical scholarship has paid less attention to the role that gender plays in the restoration material than in the oracles of doom, in part because the idyllic pictures are less problematic for contemporary audiences.

In addition, there are even fewer explicit references to women in this material, although many of the texts assume the restoration of whole communities. As a result, women are even more invisible in the restoration material.

We have already noted the gender-inclusive perspective of Isaiah 56, but where else can gender diversity be found in these texts, and do these Israelite utopias contain elements of gender justice? Most texts do not include a restructuring of gendered roles in their ideal world. The assumption seems to be that God will restore the righteous or purified male elite who will reestablish the gender norms at work in their own traditions. Given the way war and conquest decimated elite families, damaged women and children, and left the ruling elite feeling helpless, it is no wonder that their idea of perfection is a stable status quo. The condemnation of foreign marriages in Malachi 2:11 shows that one of the issues facing the postexilic community was communal identity. Foreign marriages threatened the integrity of that identity, based as it was on concepts of biological procreation. This passage also shows that one way that identity was maintained was through the continued vilification of foreign women.

Another difficulty in analyzing gender in the restoration material is the enigmatic meaning of two texts that do explicitly mention women. One is in Zechariah 5:7–11, part of a series of visions related to the restoration of Judah. In this passage, the prophet sees a woman in a basket borne by two more women who are flying it through the air to Mesopotamia (Shinar). The identity of the three women remains cause for debate, but the text explicitly identifies the central woman as a personification of evil. Thus, once again, a biblical passage uses gender and ethnicity as a metaphor for evil.

The personification of the city as a woman also appears in restoration visions. For example, the author personifies the city as Rachel in Jeremiah 31:20. This one short verse resonates with maternal pathos. First, she presents a clear picture of who Ephraim is to her: her precious and delightful baby. Then she hints that she cannot get over his loss, talking about him again and again. The verse ends with her "belly" or her uterus yearning for him, tying her love to this visceral response of a mother. The language opens up a brief glimpse into the pain of the mothers who had lost children in this war, literally giving them a voice. The image is followed in verse 22 with an enigmatic image that must have resonated with the original audience, but that makes little sense to us today. The verse states that the exiles should return because the restoration will be like nothing they have seen before. The passage then gives an image of reversal: a woman encompassing (NRSV) or surrounding a warrior. It is not clear what this means, but whatever the image is supposed to connote, it uses an image of gender reversal to represent an unexpected joyous reversal.

INTERSECTIONAL READINGS OF
PROPHETIC TEXTS

The prophetic collections have been both a source of strength as well as a cause for consternation among various groups of contemporary readers. It is impossible to provide a complete survey of the many ways those seeking gender equity from around the globe have interpreted these texts, so a few representative examples must suffice to illustrate the interpretation of prophetic texts from the perspective of intersecting identities. These interpretive stances are sometimes referred to as contextual theologies, because these scholars intentionally interpret biblical texts from their own contemporary social contexts. This includes both how the contexts of contemporary marginalized groups find parallels with the social setting of the biblical texts, as well as reinterpreting how texts have been used by dominant groups to justify continued marginalization.

Contextual theologies have had a significant impact on feminist biblical scholarship. In general, feminist scholars aim to be aware of the intersectionality of their own perspective. These intersections are not just formed through race or ethnicity, but also through gender identity and economic class. These lenses have advanced scholarship on the prophets, in no small part because they have helped raise awareness of the ethnic, gender, and class categories of the ancient world. These studies have shown that every biblical figure plays out their literary role through this great web of intersecting identities. Ezekiel is portrayed not just as a prophet; he is a male, heteronormative, elite priest who has experienced forced migration that has led to his renegotiation of his various identities. He has lost his hereditary elite position, his means of production within the ritual system, his home and, at the end, his wife, and, as such, he becomes the representative of the Babylonian exiles. Jeremiah is a male, gender-nonconforming, internally displaced priest, who experiences the fall of Jerusalem and becomes an unwilling refugee who must renegotiate these identities. His portrayal makes him the ideal survivor, who embodies the lament and suffering of those who witnessed this national tragedy. These analyses could have only arisen through the work of feminist and contextual biblical scholars bringing together these important social categories.

In the Americas, two of the most impactful contextual feminist stances have been *mujerista* theology, coming from Latina and Hispanic women both in Latin America and the United States, and womanist theology, or African American feminism. Soon after the rise of second wave feminism in the early 1970s, theologians in Latin America began to interpret biblical texts from their experience of the ongoing effects of colonization, including widespread systemic poverty and cultural annihilation. As with many of these theologies, the early pioneers were male scholars, in part because in marginalized communities women had greater barriers to attaining advanced degrees than men. One of the basic tenets of liberation theology is that the God of the Bible, including the Old Testament, is one who works for real-world liberation of oppressed groups from unjust tyranny. Although the book of Exodus provided a major lynchpin for this concept of preferential option for the poor, so too did the prophetic books, especially Amos and Micah. Although both Amos and Micah refer to the possibility of violent devastation, these two prophetic books focus on economic and social injustice within Israel and Judah itself.

Today, liberation theology informs the approach to biblical interpretation of scholars around the globe, including many feminist interpreters. While these interpreters are critical of biblical texts that support unjust oppression, they seek to lessen the impact of these texts, in light of the stronger biblical portrayal of God as concerned with the plight of the poor. Although not primarily a scholar of the prophets, the work of Ada María Isasi-Díaz provides the contours of a *mujerista* biblical interpretation utilizing key concepts from liberation theology. Primary among these is the role that *praxis*, or the lived experience of readers, must play in any interpretation centered on the oppressed. For her, the life of Latina women is an essential component of a biblical theology of liberation.[4]

Within the United States, African American communities have

4. Ada María Isasi-Díaz, *Mujerista Theology: A Theology for the Twenty-first Century* (Maryknoll, NY: Orbis, 1996).

also had a vibrant tradition of biblical interpretation, even though it has not always been represented in the scholarship of the dominant academic culture. During the nineteenth century, slaves reconfigured the Christianity of their masters through their preaching and singing in unrecognized places of worship, such as hush harbors. The lyrics of traditional spirituals reflected this interpretive tradition. Biblical womanist scholar Cheryl Kirk-Duggan has examined the theologies of African American music, from spirituals to hip-hop in a number of publications.[5]

The rise of the civil rights movement in the 1960s included a lively debate among African American leaders around religious identity. For some groups, such as the Black Panthers and the Nation of Islam, Christianity was viewed as irredeemably racist and oppressive. Others joined the global movement to reinterpret and reclaim the Bible in their search for social justice. While Martin Luther King Jr. became the voice of this movement, this public effort unrolled in concert with the beginnings of the Black Theology movement.

Black feminists, or womanists, also joined in this work, pointing out that much of the feminist biblical scholarship up until then had been carried out by and served the interests of elite white women. Their work has changed the direction of feminist biblical scholarship by their engagement with the intersectionality of race, class, and gender in both the contemporary world and the ancient world. Within prophetic studies, one of the most groundbreaking womanist biblical scholars is Renita Weems, who has made a compelling case that the prophetic marriage metaphor has contributed to the continued tolerance of domestic and sexual violence.[6]

Womanist and *mujerista* biblical interpretation are not the only feminist contextual stances. For example, ethnic Chinese American biblical scholar Gale Yee has made significant contributions to the analysis of the intersection of race, class, and gender in prophetic texts by using a materialist analysis of prophetic texts.[7] Today, the voices of feminist biblical scholars from Africa, Korea, India, and China, to

5. Cheryl Kirk-Duggan, "Sacred and Secular in African-American Music," in *The Oxford Handbook of Religion and the Arts*, ed. Frank Burch Brown (Oxford: Oxford University Press, 2014), 498–521.

6. Renita Weems, *Battered Love: Marriage, Sex and Violence in the Hebrew Bible*, OBT (Minneapolis: Fortress Press, 1995).

7. Gale A. Yee, *Poor Banished Children of Eve: Women as Evil in the Hebrew Bible* (Minneapolis: Fortress Press, 2003).

name just a few locations, are a vital part of an increasingly more global field of scholarship on the prophets.

Racial/ethnic identity is not the only aspect of identity with which gender intersects. One increasingly important lens comes from the interdisciplinary field of trauma theory. Trauma theory reads the prophetic material through the lens of individual and collective trauma. This approach has had a significant impact on interpretation of the exilic prophets Jeremiah and Ezekiel. Kathleen O'Connor has conducted groundbreaking analysis of the book of Jeremiah from this perspective, noting that one of the effects of trauma is the inability of survivors to find words adequate to describe their experiences. Recovering the language to describe trauma is an important step to recovery and reintegration of the experience. Read in this way, the book of Jeremiah provides survivors with words and images that honestly reflect their experience.[8]

Jewish feminist biblical interpretation perhaps best represents the intersectionality of all biblical interpretation. Jewish identity itself is a complex and varying mix of ethnic and religious identity. From the religious perspective alone, basic assumptions about the interpretation of the Tanakh (the Jewish term used for these Scriptures) vary among various communities. Reform Jews, a large group in the United States, would not read the Tanakh as literally true, nor would they read the laws in the Torah (or Pentateuch) as valid for all Jews at all times. This differs sharply from Orthodox Jews, who do view these laws as still valid. But even with these differences, feminist approaches within Jewish biblical interpretation have been prolific and significant over the past forty years. Perhaps one of the most influential Jewish feminist scholars is Athalya Brenner, editor for the Feminist Companion to the Bible series. Within prophetic studies, Drorah Setel coined the term "porno-prophetic" to describe the combination of sexual violence and voyeurism in Hosea's use of the marriage metaphor.[9]

The broadening of feminist approaches in recent years does not mean that the work is over. There are other aspects of intersectionality barely mentioned in current biblical studies. For example, while the burgeoning field of disability studies has begun to make a mark on biblical interpretation in general, less often discussed

8. Kathleen M. O'Connor, *Jeremiah: Pain and Promise* (Minneapolis: Fortress Press, 2011).

9. Drorah Setel, "Prophets and Pornography: Female Sexual Imagery in Hosea," in *Feminist Interpretation of the Bible*, ed. Letty Russell (Oxford: Blackwell, 1985), 86–95.

is the impact of women's physical disabilities on both the production of prophetic texts as well as their interpretation. As mentioned above, women certainly suffered gendered forms of physical harm and mutilation as a wartime practice, but even without that additional bodily harm, their embodied relationship to the natural world differed significantly from that of ancient men. Women who had a physical deformity would be less likely to marry, and therefore less likely to have the protection of a patriarchal household. Childbirth would have also rendered a percentage of women permanently disabled. Fistulas, or tears between the uterus and the digestive tract that sometimes occur in delivery, would have been unfixable, leading to a permanent leakage of urine and feces, with its concomitant status of impurity. Many conditions would have led to rampant infertility, including damage during rape or childbirth as well as a constant state of near starvation. The field of prophetic studies is ripe for a more thorough examination of the intersection of disability and gender in the prophetic material.

The engagement with the prophets by a more inclusive approach to gender has reinvigorated the application of ancient texts to contemporary issues. For readers of the Bible from the dominant culture, the life of women it reflects seems to be a phenomenon relegated to the distant past. Feminism from the perspective of intersectionality reminds contemporary audiences that many women in the world today bear the same gender-based effects from patriarchy, poverty, and marginalization as biblical women. Women still die from fistulas in much of the globe, even though we now have the technology to fix the tears. Many women still endure violent rape, abusive attempts for domestic control, gender-based starvation, hypersexualization, enslavement into human trafficking, and slut shaming not just in times and lands far away, but in our own cities, neighborhoods, and homes. Contextual feminist voices remind us that the righteous anger of the prophets is still needed today.

PREACHING AND TEACHING PROPHETIC VIEWS OF GENDER

So we return to the question raised at the beginning of this chapter. How does one teach or preach the prophetic texts to contemporary audiences well aware of the intersections of gender, race, class, and ability? Do or should these texts have any ongoing function for communities of faith? As you can see from the discussion above on the urgent need for the voices of global feminist voices, I contend that these ancient texts do remain relevant, although maybe not in the way that Christianity has traditionally understood.

One of the hidden assumptions that contemporary people have about the Bible is that every text is meant to be uplifting, edifying, or admired, in a way that ignores historical or social context. If readers come to the prophets with this unexamined assumption, then interpretive problems ensue. Certainly, the prophets describe things that they expect the audience will detest. After all, that is at the heart of the prophetic function. But their analyses of the causes of the community's corruption, or the solutions that they proffer also are abhorrent to modern feminists. The challenge for those in ministerial positions is, on the one hand, to accurately explain the text from its historical context, while, on the other hand, not reinforcing the patriarchal norms that inform the text.

Another approach to the material, which is rarely engaged, is to let go of the assumptions about the purpose of the texts, and to read them with an aesthetic sensibility. Instead of coming to the texts with a theological grid into which they must fit, the reader approaches the material with an expectation to be moved by their literary artistry. This means that if the book of Lamentations evokes a profound empathy with the personified city, then that is the point of the material. Feminist theologians have long used a hermeneutics of suspicion as a feminist principle. According to Schüssler Fiorenza, "a hermeneutics of suspicion rests on the insight that all biblical texts are articulated in grammatically masculine language—a language which is embedded in a patriarchal culture, religion, and society, and which is canonized, interpreted, and proclaimed by a long line of men."[10] I would also advocate a hermeneutic of listening, because that is what these ancient witnesses ask us to do: to simply listen to their voices as they struggle with the question, Where is God when the world is on the verge of collapse? How do the most vulnerable experience God? Is a complicit God who is near in times of total social collapse better than one who is indifferent and distant? How do we use these insights to help see the plight of those experiencing

---

10. Elisabeth Schüssler Fiorenza, *But She Said: Feminist Practices of Biblical Interpretation* (Boston: Beacon, 1992), 53.

trauma, silencing, gender-based marginalization and shaming not only around the world but even in our own communities?

This is the challenge of the biblical prophets. It was their challenge 2,500 years ago and it remains a challenge today. Feminist interpretation of the biblical prophets has made the anger and urgency of the prophets relevant again, even if we in our contemporary situations would define and address the problems in ways that differ from the ancient voices. The challenge of preaching and teaching is to translate those ancient cries into contemporary language and empathy.

FOR FURTHER READING

Bauer, Angela. *Gender in the Book of Jeremiah: A Feminist-Literary Reading*. StBL 5. New York: Peter Lang, 2003.

> This rhetorical analysis of Jeremiah provides a catalog of the myriad ways the book engages language-reflecting assumptions about women and gender in the ancient world.

Gafney, Wilda C. *Daughters of Miriam: Women Prophets in Ancient Israel*. Minneapolis: Fortress Press, 2008.

> This monograph studies the variety of ways that biblical texts refer to female prophets, not only in the prophetic books, but also in narrative texts. The author places these references within the context of the ancient Near East. The book concludes with a chapter outlining rabbinic and early Christian interpretations of these texts.

Hamori, Esther. *Women's Divination in Biblical Literature: Prophecy, Necromancy and Other Arts of Knowledge*. New Haven: Yale University Press, 2015.

> Hamori expands the classical approach to biblical prophecy to include practices of divination, such as speaking with the dead and interpreting omens. This reveals far more texts that reflect women as prophets. She places these texts within the broader phenomenon of ancient prophecy and divination.

Kamionkowski, S. Tamar, and Wonil Kim, eds. *Bodies, Embodiment, and Theology of the Hebrew Bible*. LHBOTS 465. London: T&T Clark, 2010.

> A welcome new addition to the study of gender is focus on the body, which often serves as the literary canvas for gender representation. This collection of essays, which focuses on more than just prophetic texts, provides examples of how a focus on the representation of bodies in biblical texts contributes to the material's view of gender.

Maier, Christl M., and Carolyn J. Sharp, eds. *Prophecy and Power: Jeremiah in Feminist and Postcolonial Perspective*. LHBOTS 577. London: Bloomsbury, 2013.

> This collection of essays brings together the intersectionality of gender, race/ethnicity, and postcolonial analysis with a focus on the book of Jeremiah. This represents a growing focus in gender analyses of prophetic texts.

O'Brien, Julia M., and Chris Franke, eds. *The Aesthetics of Violence in the Prophets*. LHBOTS 517. New York: T&T Clark, 2010.

> The essays in this volume look at the rhetorical function and impact of violent language often found in prophetic books. Although not all of the essays engage gender analysis, the topic does address a major concern in feminist studies of prophetic texts.

Stökl, Jonathan, and Corrine Carvalho, eds. *Prophets Male and Female: Gender and Prophecy in the Hebrew Bible, the Eastern Mediterranean, and the Ancient Near East*. AIIL 15. Atlanta: Society of Biblical Literature, 2013.

> The wide-ranging essays in this collection examine the intersection of prophecy and gender not only in biblical texts, but also in the surrounding ancient cultures. The book includes an extensive bibliography for further research.

PART IV

The Writings

4.

Affirming and Contradicting Gender Stereotypes

JUDY FENTRESS-WILLIAMS
AND MELODY D. KNOWLES

INTRODUCTION

It would be easy to assume that the presentation of women in the Writings of the Hebrew Bible is stereotypical and negative. In the varied genres of this section (stories, prayers, love poems, family trees), women are maligned, confined to the household, or simply ignored. In certain ways, this assumption about the presentation of women in the Writings is accurate. Although the texts are largely anonymous, they are likely all written by men for a male audience. And they reflect their ancient socioeconomic context, in which land is largely inherited by the oldest son, wives move into their husband's household, and daughters are often left out of the genealogical record. They also reflect their ancient theological traditions in the portrayal of God usually in male images of king, judge, and warrior.

Yet even as these creative and often beautiful texts affirm traditional assumptions about sex and gender, they also stretch and even contradict such assumptions in both the human and divine arenas. Even as Ben Sira reflects the hierarchy of a fallen world, the woman in Song of Songs offers a celebratory vision of all of God's creation restored. Even as women are largely erased from the long genealogies that open the book of Chronicles, the ones who are present promote boundary crossing as a source of blessing. God appears as both king and midwife in the Psalms, and in these prayers divine power protects the most vulnerable.

As some of the latest texts of the Hebrew Bible, the Writings witness to communities affirming and yet struggling with the received tradition and women's role within it. Contemporary readers of this material are invited into a lively and meaningful dialogue around how Scripture reflects its originating contexts and simultaneously challenges them.

FEMALE PROTAGONISTS: RUTH AND ESTHER

Ruth and Esther belong to the Festival Scroll, also known as *Megilloth*, which means that these stories have a liturgical function in Judaism. As such, they invite the community to reenact and reestablish its identity when it remembers these deliverers. Esther saves the diaspora community from genocide and Ruth brings a family back from the edge of extinction, preserving the royal bloodline. These female protagonists exercise creativity in traditional roles to navigate their respective contexts so that their people can survive. Their stories create a platform for a more nuanced theology—different ways of thinking about God and what it means to be the people of God.

RUTH

The book of Ruth begins with the introduction of some of the main characters. The order of the introduction conveys the values of the society that produced the story. The patriarch, Elimelech, is introduced first, followed by his wife, Naomi, and their two sons. Naomi is in her place, as wife and mother, between the men who define her. Famine comes into the story, bringing displacement and Elimelech's death. Ruth is introduced into the story as the wife of Naomi's son, Mahlon, along with Orpah, wife of Chilion. These marriages of Israelites to foreign women are followed by barrenness and more death, tragedy upon tragedy. In fact, it is the death of the men that brings the women to the fore. Had these tragedies not been a part of the narrative, we may never have known more than Ruth's name, if that. Even as they take more prominent roles in the narrative, Naomi and Ruth are childless widows on the edges of society. Relegated to the margins, their survival is connected to their ability to figure out how to exercise power from that space.

Although the women are introduced through traditional family structures, the movements in the story that are life-giving are not so traditional. Ruth's vow to Naomi (1:16–17) has the components of a proper vow, but the actors are all wrong. Ruth the Moabite makes a vow of fidelity to her mother-in-law, invoking the personal name of Naomi's God, somewhere between Moab and Bethlehem, literally and figuratively "no man's land." On what basis does Ruth invoke YHWH's name, and is the vow valid when uttered by a Moabite woman? Ruth doesn't ask permission but "performs" the vow of fidelity and leaves Naomi with no choice but to "say no more to her." The vow reaffirms their relationship as family with its obligations. Naomi cannot disown the Moabite, and their fates are intertwined.

Because women are featured prominently in the story, the reader is introduced to the unique constraints placed upon women. We are reminded that marriage is never separated from property, and we are reminded of the incredible pressure placed on women to produce male heirs.[1] Issues of gender, such as the ability to inherit property or means of support, or a woman's ability to travel alone without the risk of being assaulted, are further complicated by the constructs of ethnicity and nationality. In Ruth, we are invited to imagine the experience of these two different women who are united by their experiences of loss and fidelity to one another and Naomi's God. However, Naomi's plight as an Israelite widow in her hometown is not the same as Ruth's, a Moabite widow in Bethlehem. Ruth's nationality and the religion that customarily accompanies it make her even more marginalized, vulnerable, and invisible. Upon their return to Bethlehem from Moab, Naomi bemoans her calamity and suffering to the women of the town, 1:20–21, without acknowledging Ruth's presence, who according to the narrator, is right there, (v. 22). If Naomi is "utterly bereft" and alone, what are we to make of Ruth's value?

In biblical narrative, meaning comes to us both from the story's content and its form (genre). In Ruth, the plot uses Ruth's vow of fidelity to Naomi and Naomi's God as the means to make her a full participant in the story. This move is supported by the comedic

---

1. Katharine Doob Sakenfeld, *Just Wives? Stories of Power and Survival in the Old Testament and Today* (Louisville: Westminster John Knox, 2003), 39.

structure and invites readers to imagine a reality where the marginalized are brought into the center.[2] In a comedy, Ruth the Moabite can demonstrate faithfulness, *hesed*, and be better to Naomi than seven sons. Here, Ruth can make her way to the threshing floor under the cover of darkness and return home with a cloak full of seed and a potential marriage contract. No one asks if the rules that allow widows and orphans to glean also extend to the despised Moabites, who are excluded from the congregation of Israel.[3] Ruth invites us to consider how one's race or ethnicity or "otherness" contributes to their story—both in terms of what they are able to do and how they are perceived. The genre interacts with the plot, offering commentary on the rules and mores of a society, critiquing them, even as the resolution of the story will return things back to order.

The comedic structure that brings the story to resolution does not conceal the reality that women's sexuality is tied to survival in this story. Children, specifically male children, are needed for the transference of property, and Naomi and Ruth have none. Naomi's plan for their survival requires that Ruth go to Boaz on the threshing floor under the cover of darkness. The location and the time of the encounter are rife with sexual innuendo and energy. In both of his encounters with Ruth (chapters 2 and 3), Boaz demonstrates great concern and kindness toward her. Is his kindness motivated by Ruth's appearance or the possibility of a sexual encounter? The pressing issue of fertility matters greatly in this story, and sexuality is the undercurrent that doesn't go away.

Boaz marries Ruth and she gives birth to a son named Obed. Ruth now is fully a part of the Israelites.[4] In fact, she and Boaz are ancestors of Israel's beloved King David. So, the covenant that Ruth made with Naomi in chapter 1 and with Boaz in chapter 4, and the birth of Obed, have moved Ruth from the category of foreigner to family, and her presence in the family changes its constitution. The survival of Elimelech's family results from a more inclusive definition of family.

The concluding chapter offers us mixed messages. On the one hand, blessings that are given to Ruth place her in the company of the ancestresses Rachel, Leah, and Tamar. The language suggests a

2. Judy Fentress-Williams, *Ruth* (Nashville: Abingdon, 2012), 18.
3. Fentress-Williams, *Ruth*, 18.
4. Kirsten Nielson, *Ruth* (Louisville: Westminster John Knox, 1997), 93.

restoration. However, the words of blessing take place in the same chapter where the child is transferred from his birth mother to the older, established Israelite woman. Ruth gives birth to Obed, and then the child is placed on Naomi's bosom as the women celebrate, "a son has been born to Naomi (4:17)." This can be seen as the ultimate act of inclusion. However, women in minority groups are all too familiar with appropriation of their work, their knowledge, their art, and even their children by women in dominant cultures. When our acceptance of the outsider demands their absorption to the point where they disappear, we are condoning appropriation.

Many readers observe that although the book is named after Ruth, it could have been named for Naomi. She is the Israelite woman who leaves Bethlehem "full" only to return empty and experience God's redemption through the unlikely agency of a foreign woman. And she is the "mother" of Obed. However, the fact that the story bears Ruth's name is one of its victories. Ruth is more than a foreign widow in need of redemption. She is the one who facilitates the family's survival. The remembrance of the Moabitess stands as testimony against our tendencies to either exclude, ignore, or gloss over the foreigner, which allows the dominant culture to believe that they are special and that their call is exclusive.

ESTHER

The setting for the story of Esther is the Jewish community in diaspora. Jews under foreign authority must keep the reality of the Persian Empire in tension with their own identity, culture, and religion. In other words, survival in this community requires "dual realities, double consciousness, and multiple identities."[5] Like the court stories in the beginning of Daniel and the Joseph story at the end of Genesis, the protagonists' survival and success depend on their ability to exercise wisdom, as they manage competing sets of rules that come from alternate realities. There is the risk of death at the hands of a foreign ruler if they find themselves on the wrong side of the law. Alternately they stand to lose their identity with too much assimilation, and this is another kind of death.

In Esther, we observe that navigating the separate worlds of the court tales is exacerbated by gender. There is the women's realm

5. Judy Fentress-Williams, "Esther," in *The Old Testament and Apocrypha*, ed. Gale A. Yee, Hugh A. Page Jr., and Matthew J. M. Coomber (Minneapolis: Fortress Press, 2014), 487.

and the men's. The first eight verses of Esther open with the king's banquet, which is for men. Following the great detail of the first eight verses with its opulence and excess is verse 9: "Furthermore, Queen Vashti gave a banquet for the women in the palace of King Ahasuerus." Queen Vashti is in another part of the palace with the women, and has a role in the story when the "king was merry with wine" (1:10). He commands that Vashti be brought "before the king, wearing the royal crown in order to show the people and the officials her beauty" (1:11). Women are depicted as existing apart from, but for, men. Their appearance/beauty is valued, as is their obedience. Vashti's refusal to come at the king's request enrages him, and the king's advisors are concerned about how Vashti's refusal will lead to the rebellion of other wives, and "there will be no end of contempt and wrath!" (1:18b). They suggest:

> If it pleases the king, let a royal order go out from him, and let it be written among the laws of the Persians and the Medes, so that it may not be altered, that Vashti is never again to come before King Ahasuerus; and let the king give her royal position to another who is better than she. (1:19)

Esther's role in the story is tied to the queen's fate in chapter 1. She is introduced after Vashti is deposed, as Mordecai's cousin, an orphan, who is "fair and beautiful." The method used to select the new queen is closer to sex trafficking than a beauty pageant. Beautiful young virgins are corralled and placed in the king's harem. One will be selected as queen and the rest will remain in the king's second harem as concubines until or unless he calls for them by name!

Esther's beauty and obedience contribute to her success. When Esther is taken along with the other "beautiful young virgins," she wins the favor of Hegai, who has charge of the women. Esther follows the recommendations of Hegai, the chief custodian of the women. She is also obedient to her cousin Mordecai, who instructs her not to "reveal her people or her kindred" (2:10). In addition to her beauty and obedience, Esther's ascension to the throne is predicated in part on passing, allowing the dominant culture to believe she is "one of them," and enjoying the privilege that comes from being an insider.

Haman's plan to annihilate the Jews is the catalyst that forces Esther to risk her security for the well-being of her people. When Esther first heard of the decree to kill all Jews (4:4), she is "deeply distressed," but Mordecai challenges her to risk her relative safety to take action, suggesting she came to a position of influence so that she could be an advocate for the powerless (4:13). From Mordecai's perspective, Esther's privilege is for a purpose.

Critical moments in the story of Esther are associated with feasting, drinking, and festival.[6] It should come as no surprise that the plot is brought to resolution with banquets. After risking her life by coming before the king without an invitation, Esther requests simply that the king and Haman attend a banquet (5:4). When the king asks her what it is that she wants, she invites the king and Haman to a second banquet (5:7). The suspense works dramatically to set Haman up for his demise. He believes the second invitation is a sign of his increased status and honor when in reality, it is the prelude to his end. The two banquets also serve as another example of Esther exercising wisdom by using available tools of the dominant culture to save the vulnerable.

The constant vulnerability of the people in the diaspora is symbolized by the characters of Esther and her predecessor, Vashti. Both women are brought to a court where their job is to serve at the pleasure of a mercurial king. They each must navigate their way around the dictates of the powerful and foolish monarch. Thus, instead of viewing them as foils, as commentaries often do, the role of "queen" can represent the nation in exile whose fate seemingly rests in the hands of someone else.

The court tale of Esther uses some of the same motifs we find in the court narratives in Daniel and even that of Joseph (in Genesis). Esther comes into the court in a different role than that of her male counterparts in Genesis and Daniel to the king. Joseph is good-looking, but in the end, comes to power for his ability to interpret dreams and the wisdom he demonstrates. Daniel and his comrades are described as handsome, but also possessing "wisdom, knowledge and insight, and competent to serve in the king's palace" (Dan 1:4). Although she is chosen for her beauty, not for her "wisdom, knowledge and insight," it is Esther's wisdom that enables her to use the space available to her (the banquet) to influence the world of men and thwart Haman. In dialogue with the other court tales, the story of Esther reminds us that the abilities and virtues of Daniel, Joseph, Shadrach, Meshach, and Abednego are not any different from

---

6. Kenneth Craig, *Reading Esther: A Case for the Literary Carnivalesque* (Louisville: Westminster John Knox, 1995), 33.

Esther's. The characteristics they possess are those of which the king has need and they must use their abilities to survive.

WOMEN AND SEXUALITY: SONG OF SONGS
AND BEN SIRA

The Song of Songs and Ben Sira are both collections of writings that offer powerful, albeit divergent images of women and sexuality. The wisdom writings in Ben Sira/Sirach are practical teachings, deeply rooted in a specific cultural context. The Song of Songs is a collection of love poetry that transcends time and space through metaphor. As a result, the two offer radically different perspectives on the sexuality of women.

BEN SIRA/SIRACH/ECCLESIASTICUS

From a woman sin had its beginning, and because of her we all die.
—Sirach 25:24

Sirach introduces us to a world that is rooted in the hierarchy of a fallen world and is supported by a culture of male privilege. Arguably "the most misogynistic . . . among the books of the Bible,"[7] Sirach's collected wisdom comes to us from a cultural construct of honor and shame, resulting from the layering of Greek culture on Judaism. The worldview behind the book assumes that there is no life after death, and that the closest one can get to eternal life is to establish a name and reputation that will last for generations to come.[8]

Like many other collections of wisdom, Sirach is intended for a male audience. Honor is something that only men can attain, and women are commodities that can be conduits or impediments to men's success.[9] In this book of wisdom, women exist in the roles of wife, mother, daughter, and sexual object. The woman/wife is a clearly a possession, and the way she honors or dishonors her husband is tied to the way she manages the household and her sexual fidelity.[10]

---

7. Pamela Eisenbaum, "Sirach," in *Women's Bible Commentary*, ed. Carol A. Newsom, Sharon H. Ringe, and Jacqueline E. Lapsley (Louisville: Westminster John Knox, 2012), 410.
8. Michael D. Coogan, *The Old Testament* (Oxford: Oxford University Press, 2014), 509.
9. Eisenbaum, "Sirach," 411.
10. Eisenbaum, "Sirach," 411.

In this world, there are only two types of women; good women are the ones who bring honor to their husbands and bad women do not.

The ordered and hierarchical world of Ben Sira depends on women and men occupying separate spheres. The family structure is narrowly defined with men on top and women in supporting roles. In this world, daughters are burdens because their very existence creates opportunities for shame. They can be barren or disagreeable wives or unchaste daughters or unmarried (Sir 49:9–10). This worldview offers an image of woman as morally, intellectually, *and* physically weaker than men, demanding constant oversight and control. Both women and men can bring shame, but only men can achieve honor.[11] In Sirach, much of women's weakness is tied to their sexuality. Therefore, women's sexuality is to be controlled (feared) at all costs.

The separation of woman and man is justified by a hierarchy that is in turn justified by women's inferiority. The writings in Sirach go to great lengths to preserve this worldview, resulting in "wisdom" that claims an evil man is better than a good woman, prioritizing gender over character, or worse yet, ascribing character to gender.

Sirach's view of women and their sexuality is difficult to read. Placing this wisdom material in its context helps us to navigate the misogynistic writings as a perspective that comes from a particular moment and place in history. Understanding what was at stake (this construct of honor) allows us to observe how the hierarchy was created and supported. Understanding the context of these writings also helps us to respond to present-day hierarchies, particularly those that appropriate religion in an attempt to protect some concocted sense of piety or honor.

SONG OF SONGS

Opening with the words, "Let him kiss me with the kisses of his mouth," the Song of Songs calls attention to itself, both because of its beauty, and because of its inclusion in the biblical canon. The language is sensual, lush, and stunningly beautiful. At times, the descriptions are like a heavy perfume, overpowering the reader. The "Most Excellent of Songs"[12] is an extended and unapologetic

---

11. Coogan, *The Old Testament*, 514.
12. Renita Weems, *Just a Sister Away* (San Diego: Lura Media, 1988), 263.

dialogue between a woman and a man that explores the depths of love and the power of longing and desire. It appears to have "no theological purpose beyond itself, making no mention of God."[13] In this way, it exists seemingly unaware of the cultural limitations placed on women, evoking that moment in primordial time when the man and the woman were "naked" and "unashamed." Perhaps it harkens back to the garden of Eden, or looks forward to a time when such restrictions do not exist.

Of the two protagonists, it is the woman that commands our attention. Unnamed, twice she is referred to as "the Shulamite," the meaning of which is not clear.[14] She describes herself as "black and beautiful," a result of having been forced to work in the sun. The decision to translate the phrase "black and beautiful" versus "black but beautiful" has been a point of great interest for people of color. If she is darker than most because she is working in the fields, then the *waw* should be translated as "but," suggesting contrast between what she is and what she should be. Implicit in this interpretation is the correlation between skin color and class and the idea that people of the upper class do not work out in the sun and would be of lighter skin. (Consider the derogatory term "redneck" in the southern United States.) If her working in the fields is to be read metaphorically, could she be referring to her ancestor Ham? Ham was cursed by his father Noah to be "lowest of slaves . . . to his brothers" (Gen 9:25) and was associated with Cush (Ethiopia) and Egypt, lands in northern Africa. If translated this way, she could be referring to her skin color as something she "inherited" in the past, in which case she would be black and beautiful. Finally, how do we understand "dark" skin in this context? Is this "insider talk" for people of color? She is black, but what is the default color? What matters for many dark readers is the coexistence of darkness and beauty in worlds and societies where the two are not expected to coexist. Women of color celebrate the beauty of this dark woman, regardless of how she came to her color, because she holds a place where darker women can see themselves in the biblical text in a positive light.

The woman is young and passionate. She is unashamed of her love and her lover and is driven by her desire to be united with him. She

---

13. Hannah Matis, "Song of Songs," in *The CEB Women's Bible*, ed. Jaime Clark-Soles, Judy Fentress-Williams, Ginger Gaines-Cirelli, Christine Chakoian, and Rachel Baughman (Nashville: Abingdon: 2015), 850.

14. Chana Bloch, "Woman/Lover/Shulammite," in *Women in Scripture*, ed. Carol Meyers (Boston: Houghton Mifflin, 2000), 311.

is self-possessed and bold, the "embodiment of erotic pleasure."[15] Her beauty is celebrated and she is distinguished by her "assertiveness."[16] She and her lover use metaphorical language to express themselves. For that reason, there is something about the *Song of Songs* that defies time and space. Geographic locations are used, but not accurately or consistently. Multiple references are made to gardens as locations, and she herself at some point becomes a garden. Time is at the service of the lovers' experience, so it is clearly something other than a "historical" account. Geography is flexible and chronology optional. The metaphorical language does not take us away from the physical realm but is employed to celebrate the mysterious joys of embodiment.

What then, is the purpose of this poetry? Is it simply to celebrate love? Is it ultimately to draw us to God, and if so, in what way? The allegorical possibilities are well known. Both Judaism and Christianity have seen in the song an expression of love between God and God's people and Christ and the church. Symbolic language easily lends itself to such interpretations. However, interpretations that rush to describe the poetry as allegorical can lead the reader away from the intensity of the sexual longing. The song's emphasis on desire attests to its ability to overtake and possess us. Any allegorical reading must preserve the sense that the connection we have with the Creator is passionate and disorienting.

The poetry of the Song of Songs also forms a dialogue with the very first story in Genesis. Phyllis Trible makes a compelling argument that the Song of Songs is a remix of the story of the garden of Eden revisited. In the Song of Songs, the "post-fall" hierarchy and male dominance are gone. What remains is the simple love between the two, unfettered by the limits of a sinful world. In response to the punishment in the post-Edenic world of Genesis 3, where the woman is told she will bear children "in pain . . . yet your desire shall be for your husband and he shall rule over you" (Gen 3:16), the Song of Songs offers a reversal when the woman states, "my beloved is mine and his desire is for me." She is not called a wife, and bearing children is not required.[17] Rather, Trible argues the Song of Songs celebrates "love for the sake of love." It is a celebration of humanity that invites us to recognize and enjoy our "creatureliness." With the opening and

15. Bloch, "Woman/Lover/Shulammite," 310.

16. Bloch, "Woman/Lover/Shulammite," 311.

17. Phyllis Trible, "Love's Lyrics Redeemed," in *God and the Rhetoric of Sexuality* (Philadelphia: Fortress Press, 1978), 162.

closing words to the song, it is the woman who bids us to taste and experience and know.

WOMAN WISDOM IN THE WISDOM BOOKS: PROVERBS, JOB, WISDOM OF SOLOMON

Biblical wisdom is intended for a male audience. Proverbs consists of the words of a father to his son, a younger man, as an introduction to the way of wisdom. The book of Job is about a man who wrestles with the limits of wisdom, and the Wisdom of Solomon is a reflection on philosophical ideas.[18] The male focus can result in a skewed perspective, creating a literary world where women are metaphors, symbols, appendages, objects, and possessions. However, the consistent personification of wisdom as feminine in this tradition offers a countertradition, another way of reading, for fruitful dialogue.[19]

PROVERBS

The Proverbs of Solomon are an introduction to the wisdom tradition. Deceptive in their simplicity, the teachings in Proverbs are didactic. There is a right and wrong way, a wise and foolish young man, and the virtuous woman is contrasted with the wanton woman (7:4–5). The father instructs the son in the ways of wisdom, urging him to choose wisdom as "sister" and "intimate friend" (7:4), but to avoid the strange woman who leads men "without sense" (7:7) to destruction. But in Proverbs, the father's teachings are not the only voice. Wisdom speaks directly to her audience of young men, establishing her authority, which comes from her origins and role in creation.

> The Lord created me at the beginning of his work,
> the first of his acts long ago. (8:22)

Chapter 8 of Proverbs is an iconic text, drawing a picture of Wisdom that leads us to know more about God. With her direct speech,

---

18. John J. Collins, *A Short Introduction to the Hebrew Bible* (Minneapolis: Fortress Press, 2014), 360.

19. For more on countertraditions, see Ilana Pardes, *Countertraditions in the Bible: A Feminist Approach* (Cambridge, MA: Harvard University Press, 1992).

Wisdom is established as something more than a literary motif. Exactly what defines the "something more" is a subject for debate. The verb in Proverbs 8:22 that is translated as "created" can also mean "brought forth." Is Wisdom a part of the created order or something that was already there, coexisting with God? Wisdom also speaks to her place in creation, alongside God: "when he marked out the foundations of the earth, then I was beside him, like a master worker" (vv. 29b–30a). The term "master worker/artisan" can also be translated as "child/darling,"[20] leading us to wonder, is Wisdom a creation or co-creator? Is it Wisdom that God addresses in Genesis 1:26 when he says, "Let us make humankind in our image and according to our likeness"? Is Wisdom a part of God?

What is clear is that Wisdom has authority by her longevity and role in creation. Wisdom's presence in the primordial world means that she is in the very fiber of the created order and her imprint is everywhere. She, whether created or co-creator, is linked to the Creator and is an active participant in the maintenance of the world. It is from this place of authority and seniority that Wisdom calls the audience to obedience, "for whoever finds me finds life" (8:35). In the world outside of Eden, it is in following Wisdom that humanity can have long, if not eternal life.

The final chapter of Proverbs offers a different icon of women and wisdom. Chapter 31:10–31 is an acrostic poem, meaning that the first verse begins with the first letter and each successive verse begins with the successive letter of the Hebrew alphabet. It is the "*aleph* to *tav*" or "a to z" of the ideal wife.[21] She is described as a woman of valor, virtue, or strength. This woman benefits her husband in the same way that wisdom brings riches and honor and long life to those who possess her. The man who marries the worthy, capable, strong woman demonstrates his own wisdom by choosing her. Although the wife in Proverbs 31 is not Lady Wisdom, she is the idealized and earthly version of wisdom and the man who selects her is also wise.

The image of the ideal wife in Proverbs 31 is limiting for many contemporary readers in that her value is tied to her ability to serve, support, and bring honor to her family. Since both English words, "woman" and "wife," come from the same Hebrew term, is there

---

20. Roland Murphy uses the terms "artisan" and "darling" in *The Tree of Life: An Exploration of Biblical Wisdom Literature* (Grand Rapids: Eerdmans, 1990), 18.

21. The word for woman in Hebrew also means wife. Here it is safe to say this woman is functioning in the role of wife.

room in the Wisdom tradition for other models of virtue or strength? How can contemporary interpreters of Scripture find ways to expand the definition of the ideal woman?

JOB

The wife of Job is well known as a foil for her husband, who is the paragon of faith in the wisdom book that bears his name. If Proverbs is our introduction to Wisdom, the book of Job points to the limits of wisdom. Job's suffering challenges the teaching of Proverbs that promises long life, riches, and rewards for following Wisdom by obeying the Torah. While Job patiently endures his afflictions, his wife asks the question that begs to be asked: "Do you still persist in your integrity? Curse God and die" (2:9). Job's reprimand of his wife, in which he calls her a "foolish woman," places her on the wrong side of the didactic world of wisdom. Traditionally she is condemned for attempting to lead Job into sin. Some scholars have revisited the exchange between Job and his wife, offering another way of understanding this woman. Focusing on the word "integrity," Ilana Pardes suggests that Job's wife "prefigures . . . the impatience of the dialogues."[22] Her challenge that his behavior is pious but not authentic gets to the undercurrent in the story. Her question opens the door for an authentic dialogue with a just God, who does not appear to be following the rules. In a book that explores the limits of wisdom, Job's wife advocates for an honest relationship with the deity. In this sense, she is a wife who pushes her husband to a deeper understanding of wisdom.[23] This understanding is rooted not in the simple cause and effect of Proverbs but in relationship with a deity who is beyond our understanding.

WISDOM OF SOLOMON

The apocryphal book Wisdom of Solomon reflects the influence of Greek culture and philosophy and offers an image of Woman Wisdom that is "developed and elevated to an unparalleled degree."[24]

22. Pardes, *Countertraditions in the Bible*, 147.

23. Carol Newsom, "Job," in *Women's Bible Commentary*, ed. Carol A. Newsom, Sharon H. Ringe, and Jacqueline E. Lapsley (Louisville: Westminster John Knox, 2012), 210.

24. Claudia Camp, "Woman Wisdom in the Apocryphal/Deuterocanonical Books," in *Women in Scripture*, ed. C. Meyers (Boston: Houghton Mifflin, 2000), 551.

In Wisdom of Solomon, the description of Wisdom is developed in such a way that the lines defining categories of deity, human, and spirit are blurred. The author uses the metaphor of relationship/ marriage to describe his relationship with Wisdom. Sometimes Wisdom behaves like a wife and sometimes she acts like a goddess. Influenced by the Egyptian goddess Isis, it is difficult to distinguish Wisdom from God:[25]

> For she is a breath of the power of God,
> and a pure emanation of the glory of the Almighty;
> Therefore nothing defiled gains entrance into her
> for she is a reflection of the eternal light,
> a spotless mirror of the working of God,
> and an image of his goodness. (7:25–26)

The wisdom tradition may be rooted in a male-oriented world, but the personification of Wisdom is an alternative lens, which offers a spectrum of possibilities for the "ways of Wisdom," and invites us into the mysteries of God.

GOD AND WOMEN AND THE PSALMS

My God, my God, why have you forsaken me?

—(Ps 22:1)

As you read the prayer above, who do you imagine the speaker to be? And as you read through the entire Psalter, what image does it construct of the "ideal" speaker? And who is the God that is reflected in these words?

For millennia, people of faith have looked to see their lives reflected in the Psalms, and they have been encouraged to turn to these texts to give voice to their experience and to have their experience shaped by these prayers. But the assumption that every human life is (or should be) fully embraced by these ancient texts must be examined with a critical eye. Long associated with the warrior king David, and reflecting the ancient mores of a subsistence Mediterranean economy, the careful interpreter will want to consider what values these texts promote and whose voices they represent. How might these pious texts be used to inscribe dominant values on the

---

25. Camp, "Woman Wisdom in the Apocryphal/Deuterocanonical Books," 550–51.

nondominant members of society? And where might these ancient prayers still provide resources for liberation?

To begin unpacking some of these questions, it is critical to examine the way the Psalter presents both God and women in order to see the possibilities and problems involved in adopting the words of the text. And given the Psalter's particular history of reception and use over the ages, tracing some of this history will provide perspective and prospects for current use.

GOD IN THE PSALMS

The most common images for God in the Psalter are related to the male and socially authoritative roles of king, warrior, and judge. Yet, not only does the book include additional nonmale imagery for God, it also upends and redefines gender categories on both the human and divine levels. In Psalm 22, for example, the distressed psalmist calls upon God to respond and to rescue. At first, God is "the holy one" (Ps 22:3), above and beyond all human categories. And yet, even as the psalmist moves out of male and even human categories ("I am a worm, not even a man!" (22:6), the author imagines God as a midwife: "You are the one who pulled me from the womb, placing me safely at my mother's breasts" (22:9). This relation of God to birth and the birthing process occurs at several points in the Psalms, with images of God knitting humans together in the womb (139:13), "birthing" creation into being (90:2), and having at core the attribute of "mercy," a term related to the word for "womb" (Ps 25:6; 40:11, etc.). In the context of Psalm 22, there is a sense in which the "birthing" that God supports is an inner transformation of the self in which the borrowed language of traditional religion becomes "internally persuasive" and liberating.[26] In the concluding praise, the psalmist continues this upending, lauding the holy midwife God as over and above all human authority, the one whom "all the earth's powerful will worship" (22:29).

Contemporary analysis also considers individual Psalms within their placement in the book. Thus, a full perspective on the image

---

26. For an analysis of this inner transformation in which the divine midwife is the agent, see L. Juliana M. Claassens, "Rupturing God-Language: The Metaphor of God as Midwife in Psalm 22," in *Engaging the Bible in a Gendered World: An Introduction to Feminist Biblical Interpretation in Honor of Katharine Doob Sakenfeld*, ed. Linda Day and Carolyn Pressler (Louisville: Westminster John Knox, 2006), 166–75.

of God in Psalm 22 must study how it is supported or supplanted by Psalms 21 and 23. In the present ordering of the Psalter, the divine midwife and world-worshiped king of Psalm 22 stands alongside both the shepherd in Psalm 23 who tends to the daily needs of a single sheep as well as the avenging destroyer of Psalm 21. A full assessment of God in Psalm 22 would want to see how the images work within their current literary context.

Outside of Psalm 22, the imagery for God in the Psalter continues to confirm and confound gender stereotypes, with divine power often used for the benefit of the weak. God as "king" and "Lord of Hosts" in Psalm 84 provides a home for sparrows and swallows. God as "judge" and "destroyer" in Psalm 94 is called upon to use this power against those who kill widows, immigrants, and orphans. God as "helper" (a term in the Hebrew Bible that is used only for God and women, never for men) supports the orphans (Ps 10:14).[27]

It would not be honest to claim that the Psalter fully transcends all patriarchal assumptions when it talks about God. Yet in its openness to interrogate the status quo and to use power on behalf of the weak, there is much in this text to resource strategies of liberation and change.

WOMEN IN THE PSALMS

At points, women appear in the texts of the Psalms either supporting the poetry or enacting the customs of their time. The central feature of parallelism means that the lines of every verse must balance, so sometimes women appear simply to provide poetic ballast, as in: "I have become a stranger to my own brothers, an immigrant to my mother's children" (Ps 69:8). At other points, the presentation of women portrays the social and religious customs of ancient Israel. The prayer in Psalm 144 ("May our sons in their youth be like plants fully grown, our daughters like corner pillars cut for the building of a palace") reflects the practice of women working indoors while men worked outside and the hope that all children flourish into healthy adulthood (Ps 144:12). The instruction that a new bride forget her people and bow before her groom and master (Ps 45:10–11) relates to the practice of women leaving their family's house to join their husbands' households upon marriage. Portraying Jerusalem as the

27. See the description of Eve, Abigail, and wives in Gen 2:18, 20; 1 Sam 25:41; and Sir 36:29.

birthplace of the world in Psalm 87 stems from the ancient tradition that cities are female, often the wife of the chief god.[28] In the context of worship, women members of the congregation are specifically called upon to sing in certain Psalms (i.e., "Praise YHWH . . . young men and young women," Ps 148:12), linking up with other biblical texts where women led victory songs of praise (Exod 15:20; Judg 11:34; 1 Sam 18:6; Jer 31:4).[29]

It may be that some of the Psalms are most fully understood when read as the prayers of ancient women. Indeed, the complicated Hebrew grammar is cleared up when Psalm 131:2 is read in the woman's voice: "I'm like the weaned child that is with me."[30] Of course, just as prayers written in the masculine voice can still be appropriated by women, the prayer of Psalm 131 can be taken on by men. Indeed, the final verse of the prayer invites the entire community to seek and adopt what can be learned from the maternal experience of holding one's weaned and patient child: "O Israel, wait for the Lord!" (131:3).

Either by portraying them in their ancient context or by representing their prayers, the Psalter includes women and their voices. As with the text's portrayal of God, the reader will want to examine this presentation and reflect on the tensions—how might these texts be the prayers *of women* (and expressive of their fullest humanity), and how might they be the prayers *for women* (to train them to support the power structures of the status quo)?

WOMEN USING THE PSALMS

Psalms are explicitly designed to be prayed by the readers, whether female or male. The texts usually adopt the first-person voice, such as in the plea "have mercy on me!" (Ps 6:2). They also often avoid details that bind the prayers to one particular time and place, so that opposing forces are often simply called "my enemies" (Ps 23:5), and the depictions of joy are open enough to embrace the experience of

---

28. For more on the ancient city as a woman, see Christl M. Maier, *Daughter Zion, Mother Zion: Gender, Space, and the Sacred in Ancient Israel* (Minneapolis: Fortress Press, 2008).

29. For more, see Carol Meyers, "Of Drums and Damsels: Women's Performance in Ancient Israel," *Biblical Archaeologist* 54 (1991): 16–27.

30. Melody D. Knowles, "A Woman at Prayer: A Critical Note on Psalm 131:2b," *JBL* 125 (2006): 385–89.

the current reader, as in "I will sing to the Lord, for he has been good to me" (Ps 13:6).

Given the significance of "voice" in feminist and intersectional interpretation, this feature of the Psalms is particularly significant. How does the text shape the one who reads it? Moreover, the text has a unique history of use in that over the centuries communities have encouraged women to read it and adopt the words as their own. Where might this history provide possibilities for the full flourishing of all humanity?

In addition to the internal literary features named above, the superscriptions that introduce the text also encourage the reader to apply the text to themselves or others. The association of a Psalm with an ancient figure (most often David, but some superscriptions also name Solomon, Moses, and others) means that the prayer looks beyond itself, and aims to get attached to different narratives. Often the superscriptions relate the text to specific biblical stories, so that the reader of Psalm 51 is encouraged to read the text as the prayer of David in the aftermath of his rape of Bathsheba described in 2 Samuel 12. At times, this attachment of particular stories to particular Psalms can have a narrowing effect, so that Psalm 51 is only heard in this one context and in the one male confessional voice. Yet the superscriptions have also provided license to hear various Psalms as the prayers of other women and men in addition to the one named in the superscription. Thus, for example, Psalm 22 is clearly marked as a "Psalm of David," yet Christians have long heard in it the prayer of the dying Jesus, and Jews have read it as the prayer of Esther.[31] Other more contemporary readings link Psalms to other biblical women or to the experience of women outside of the Bible. Bail, for example, reads Psalm 55 as the lament of the raped and dying woman described in Judges 19,[32] and Reinstra rewrites the superscription of Psalm 22 so that it is read as "the prayer of a Jewish woman who finally escaped a Nazi death-camp."[33]

In addition to being read as the prayers of women, the Psalms have been used as a pathway for literacy and an entrance into the biblical text itself. When asked about the optimal educational program for

31. Catherine Brown Tkacz, "Esther, Jesus, and Psalm 22," *CBQ* 70 (2008): 709–28.

32. Ulrike Bail, "'O God, Hear My Prayer': Psalm 55 and Violence against Women," in *Wisdom and Psalms*, ed. Athalya Brenner and Carole R. Fontaine, Feminist Companion to the Bible 2 (Sheffield: Sheffield Academic, 1998), 242–63.

33. Marchiene Vroon Rienstra, *Swallow's Nest: A Feminine Reading of the Psalms* (Grand Rapids: Eerdmans, 1992), 40.

a young girl, St. Jerome highlighted the primary and formative role of this text: "Let her learn the Psalter first."[34] With the rise of monasteries, reciting the Psalms was a core feature of the daily offices for both nuns and monks. In pre-Reformation Europe, lay women and men who otherwise had limited access to the biblical text said their daily prayers using "Books of Hours" that consisted primarily of Psalms.[35] Some versions come complete with a page at the beginning so children could learn to read, and then practice their reading by praying the Psalms.[36] Later, Protestants kept Psalms at the core of their piety by translating them into the vernacular and singing them in metrical paraphrase. When English Puritans settled in America, they brought with them this tradition, and a metrical paraphrase for use in worship, *The Bay Psalm Book*, was the first book printed in America in 1640. Contemporary letters from later periods also record that enslaved communities in America read and sang from the Psalter.[37]

In addition to serving as a path to literacy and the knowledge of God, portions of the text have also been used by the faithful as a way to prevent evil and sometimes even to cure sickness. As amulets, Psalm texts are either written on small pieces of paper and folded into cylinders or inscribed on metal and hung on a cord. Examples include a small papyrus from the fourth or fifth century upon which are Psalm 91:1–2 and the Lord's Prayer written in Greek.[38] Silver pendants from later periods have been found inscribed with the first letters of Psalm 121:8 along with the names of the biblical ancestors

34. Quoted by Abelard, "On Educating Virgins," in *Guidance for Women in 12th-Century Convents*, trans. Vera Morton, Library of Medieval Women (Cambridge: D. S. Brewer, 2003), 124.

35. For an introduction to the popular use of these texts, see Eamon Duffey, *Marking the Hours: English People and Their Prayers 1240-1570* (New Haven: Yale University Press, 2006).

36. As in the Bolton Hours and the Hunter primer, in Nicolas Orme, *Medieval Children* (New Haven: Yale University Press, 2001), 248–49.

37. See, for example, the letter written in eighteenth-century Virginia by the Methodist minister Samuel Davis: "The Negroes have an ear for [Musick] and a kind of [extatic] Delight in Psalmody; and there are no Books they learn so soon or take so much pleasure in as those used in that heavenly part of divine worship." Quoted in Nathaniel Samuel Murrell, "Playing with the First One Hundred Years in the Africana Experience," in *The Africana Bible: Reading Israel's Scripture from Africa and the African Diaspora*, ed. Hugh R. Page Jr. (Minneapolis: Fortress Press, 2010), 221.

38. Edmund Harris Kase Jr., ed., *Papyri in the Princeton University Collections* (Princeton: Princeton University Press, 1936), 2:102–3, no. 107; quoted in Don C. Skemer, *Binding Words: Textual Amulets in the Middle Ages* (Princeton: Princeton University Press, 2006), 84–85.

Sarah, Rachel, Abraham, and Isaac.[39] According to the inscriptions, these amulets were worn by men as well as women. Following a quotation of Psalm 91 ("You shall not be afraid of the terror of night, nor the arrow that flies by day"), one piece includes this line: "A protection to the bearer of this amulet; Benjamin son of Solomon."[40] In another example, the first letters from Psalm 128:1–6 are followed by the owner's name: "Jochebed the daughter of Zipleh."[41] This use parallels traditions where portions of specific psalms are recited along with additional prayers and holy names in contemporary African communities.[42]

Such amulets and recitations physically represent the power of the Psalms to shape the reality of women and men throughout the ages. As texts designed to be prayed and sung, they have given voice to the voiceless and restored subjecthood and identity. And as the first (and sometimes only) text read by some, they have been the vehicle into literacy and the biblical text itself. Yet their power can also be used against the weak, and their depiction of God and ancient women can be used to subjugate and exploit. Readers who are called into the words of the text, and asked to join their voice to pray "My God, my God . . ." (Ps 22:1), must bear in mind the possibilities and problems that such a prayer provokes.

WOMEN IN THE RETELLINGS OF THE NATION'S HISTORY: CHRONICLES, EZRA, NEHEMIAH, AND 1–2 MACCABEES

There is a sense in which history never stays put. Although the actual events of the past don't change, the recording of these events within a satisfying narrative is a task that is never complete. Sometimes archeological discoveries are made, and suddenly new characters and previously unknown events can be included into the account of the past. Or, more frequently, new questions are asked of the extant sources, and the narrative is modified to include new perspectives.

39. Theodore Schrire, *Hebrew Amulets: Their Decipherment and Interpretation* (London: Routledge & Kegan Paul, 1967), 157–58, pl. 30.

40. Schrire, *Hebrew Amulets*, 139–40, pl. 1.

41. Schrire, *Hebrew Amulets*, 158, pl. 31.

42. David Tuesday Adamo, "Psalm 101-150," in *The Africana Bible: Reading Israel's Scripture from Africa and the African Diaspora*, ed. Hugh R. Page Jr. (Minneapolis: Fortress Press, 2010), 229–36.

For example, when ancient texts such as the New Testament book of Romans 16:7 is examined from a contemporary feminist perspective, it emerges that Paul was greeting the woman "Junia" as one "prominent among the apostles" rather than the man "Junias," and our account of women's roles in leadership positions in the early church suddenly changes.

Such writing and rewriting accounts of the past is not a new project. The communities who worshiped YHWH in the Persian and Hellenistic periods had their own versions of the time that came before. The books of Ezra, Nehemiah, and 1–2 Maccabees provide largely unique accounts of the relatively recent (postexilic) past. In contrast, the book of 1–2 Chronicles reworks texts such as 2 Samuel and 1–2 Kings to give a new presentation of the earlier (preexilic) period. And even as these texts were canonized by later communities who heard in them the word of God for their own day, they retained and promoted assumptions concerning gender and social structures active at the time of writing.

This promotion of assumptions is particularly clear when the texts are examined for their presentation of women and their construction of communal boundaries. Who can be counted as the people of God? Who is in and who is out? And what particular dangers do women pose to the purity of this group?

These questions are given distinctive answers in these texts as the community grappled with the new political situation of the Persian Empire, in a context of imperialization and decolonization. Social demarcation had a particular urgency when the worship of YHWH could now be practiced by faithful groups who remained in diaspora throughout the empire in countries such as Egypt and Greece and Persia. And those who returned to their ancestral holdings now lived in a land where the large ideal geography of Judah and Israel that once stretched "from Dan to Beersheba" was now limited to the smaller province of Yehud. In addition, not all of the population of Yehud were considered to be part of the community, at least by some who spoke with authority in the books of Ezra and Nehemiah. In this new context, the community no longer depended on physical proximity to Jerusalem as a sure marker of belonging, but set about creating and enacting new standards for inclusion and exclusion. In addition to religious practice and belief, genealogy and geography are key considerations for communal boundaries in the biblical texts of this period.

These issues are central in all of the historical narratives that form part of the Writings in the Hebrew Bible. With the shared conviction that the people's recent experience of forced migration in the form of exile to Babylon was due to their sin (i.e., Neh 9:29–31), it was critical that the correct values were promoted. And as the contemporary reader works through these stories about Israel's past, she is wise to look for the interests and anxieties that beset the writer's community. In so doing, she will see more of the different perspectives on women and outsiders during this period, as well as the liveliness of the historical record itself.

WOMEN IN CHRONICLES

At first glance, women and outsiders in the books of Chronicles seem largely absent. In this rehearsal of the nation's mostly preexilic history, the main actors are kings, the main storyline is the reign of the firstborn male descendants of David, and the major topics are the kingship and the temple with its male priests in Jerusalem. When compared to the source texts that the author employs (2 Samuel and 1–2 Kings), all of the stories about women are excluded or considerably shortened with the exception of those about the queen of Sheba (2 Chronicles 9) and Queen Athaliah (2 Chronicles 22–23). The treatment of the stories about women in the source material mirrors the treatment of stories about those outside of the sacred territory of Jerusalem and Judah—if events happened outside of this small territory, they are largely ignored. Yet even in this context of literary excision, the text also includes certain details that indicate an openness to the role of women and foreigners as part of the people of God and agents of blessing.

This is particularly evident in the nine-chapter "genealogical vestibule"[43] that opens the book. A contemporary Western audience may be used to regarding such lists of names as simple and straightforward facts unaffected by authorial innovation or literary invention. Yet the genre is remarkably flexible and able to shape and erase and construct a past in line with particular values and commitments. Notice, for example, that in telling the story of the nations, the author begins with the genealogy of the first human family: "Adam, Seth, Enosh . . ." (1 Chr 1:1). By linking the present

43. This phrase is borrowed from Manfred Oeming, *Das Wahre Israel: Die "Genealogische Vorhalle" 1 Chronik 1-9* (Stuttgart: Kohlhammer, 1990).

community of God's people with the very first human family, the author is signaling that the nation is related to all the peoples of the earth via a shared ancestor. Careful readers will not want simply to receive this section as a fully accurate representation of the many lines of the family tree, but rather as an ideal portrayal of the past; like all histories it enshrines some values even as it disparages others, and hides as well as reveals.

Although they are largely edited out of the genealogical history, women nevertheless play a significant role at key points in these chapters. Within a literary genre that privileges the function of men in the unfolding of generations, it is notable that over forty women are also mentioned within this genealogy.[44] Some of these women have names and some do not, and all are designated by their relation to men in their lineage role. For example, Keturah is presented as the second wife of Abraham and mother of Zimran and Jokshan. (1 Chr 1:32), and Sheshan's (unnamed) daughter is presented as the wife of Jarha and mother of Attai (1 Chr 2:35). In this genre in which names are such critical elements, it is significant that those who name the children are often women (1 Chr 4:9 and 7:16).[45] It is also striking that sometimes the lineage is traced not through the male line but through the female one.[46] For example, "the sons of Zeruiah" are known by the name of their mother (1 Chr 2:16–17), and the genealogy of Hadad's wife Mehetabel is traced back three generations through her matrilineal line (1 Chr 1:50).

The positive portrayal of foreign women in the Chronicler's genealogies is especially striking given the anxieties that texts such as Ezra and Nehemiah manifest. In line with a presentation of the past that links all of the families via the shared ancestor Adam, the genealogy gives a positive presentation of foreign wives and mothers. For example, the text is clear that the family intermarried with Canaanites (Judah's wife Bath-Shua mentioned in 1 Chr 2:3), Gesherites (David's wife Maacah in 1 Chr 3:2), and Egyptians

44. The large number of women mentioned in the first nine chapters is comparable to the rest of the text—the two books of Chronicles contain the most names of women and notes about them in the whole of the Bible. See Marie-Theres Wacker, "Books of Chronicles: In the Vestibule of Women," in *Feminist Biblical Interpretation: A Compendium of Critical Commentary on the Books of the Bible and Related Literature*, ed. Luise Schottroff and Marie-Theres Wacker, trans. Lisa E. Dahill et al. (Grand Rapids: Eerdmans, 2012), 178–91, 178.

45. Outside of 1–2 Chronicles, see also Gen 4:25 and 29:33. The text also records instances of fathers naming their children, such as when Ephraim names his son Beriah in 1 Chr 7:23.

46. Noted by Antje Labahn and Ehud Ben Zvi, "Observations on Women in the Genealogies of 1 Chronicles 1–9," *Biblica* 84, no. 4 (2003): 457–78.

(Mered's wife Bithiah in 1 Chr 4:17).[47] Far from simply being a cause for religious infidelity or impurity, the Chronicler's genealogies present intermarriage as a potential source of blessing, with ethnic diversity as a means of growth for the nation.

Hidden away in these chapters is also the extraordinary mention of a female city builder, Sheerah, whose city is named after her: Uzzen-Sheerah (1 Chr 7:24). Such an attribution to a woman is unparalleled in the ancient world, where the association of city building is with men (see Gen 4:17; Josh 19:50; Judg 1:26; 1 Chr 8:12).

The treatment of women throughout the rest of the book is similarly mixed. At points, when women are named as part of the offspring of pious kings, they seem to function simply as an "ornamental confirmation of the blessing of God."[48] And when they are left out of the narrative (such as most of the stories about Bathsheba, as well as Tamar's rape by her half-brother Amnon), this seems most likely because they reflect poorly on the characters of male heroes such as David. Yet almost all of the queen mothers are named in the accounts of their sons, and the texts give new information about the significant role of women in ancient politics and the cult.

There is a sense in which the entire text of 1–2 Chronicles, for all of its difficulties, functions to destabilize the dominant version of the past. Collins refers to these books as "an alternative account" to the story given in 2 Samuel and 1–2 Kings.[49] To be sure, a contemporary reader might take issue with this presentation of the past, which often edits out women and the world outside Jerusalem. Yet at the same time, the books indicate that no one presentation of the past is adequate, and that the dominant narrative can be reshaped and retold.

WOMEN IN EZRA AND NEHEMIAH

As in the book of Chronicles, a core feature of the books of Ezra and Nehemiah is the concern to define the boundaries of the community. Even as these texts tell of the return of exiles to the land and the

---

47. Foreign men are also included via Jether the Ishmaelite (Abigail's husband in 1 Chr 2:17) and Jarha the Egyptian (Sheshan's daughter's husband in 1 Chr 2:34–35). Outside of the genealogies, note also that David's army included "valiant warriors" from the nations of the Ahohites, Hittites, and Moabites (1 Chr 11:12, 41, 46).

48. Wacker, "Books of Chronicles," 183.

49. John J. Collins, *A Short Introduction to the Hebrew Bible*, 2nd ed. (Minneapolis: Fortress Press, 2014), 283.

work of Ezra and Nehemiah, they also assert group norms and define the social categories of who is in and who is out. Most clearly and strongly, these texts highlight genealogy as well as geography as the surest markers for inclusion and exclusion.

This is especially clear in the first part of the book of Ezra, chapters 1–6. After Cyrus declares that the exiles can return to the land (Ezra 1:2–4), there is a list of names of those who went to Babylon and "returned to Jerusalem and Judah, all to their own towns" (Ezra 2:1; there is a similar list in Neh 7:6–73a). Although it is tempting to think of this list as a census of those who immediately responded to Cyrus's call, several details indicate that it is a later document pasted together from a variety of sources. Initially, the people are listed by family units (2:3–19), then by towns (2:21–35), then by vocation (2:36–57). In addition, one of the family heads has the very Persian name of "Bigvai" (Ezra 2:14). Although the people sometimes borrowed names from other ethnic groups, it is strange indeed to see this in a text coming from the first year of Persian rule. Read as a composite document from a variety of times and a variety of sources, the list witnesses to the perceived need that the community have written proof of a biological connection to members of the group, even if they weren't part of the first wave of those who returned. Members of the group who traveled back from Babylon but didn't have an entry in the record "were excluded from the priesthood as unclean" (Ezra 2:62).

Ezra 1–6 includes additional texts that maintain that genealogical descent from those who had returned from Babylon is necessary to be part of the "children of the exile." This is especially clear in encounters with other groups that the text calls "people of the land," or "adversaries." For example, when the "adversaries" claim that they are loyal Yahwists and offer to join in the project of temple building, the advance is strongly rebuffed: "You'll have no part with us in building a house for our God" (Ezra 4:1–3). The likeliest explanation for this encounter is that the returnees were approached by Israelites who did not go into exile, and their lack of exilic experience meant that they were now outside the community. Finally, at the close of this section, the community celebrates the completion of the temple with a Passover festival (Ezra 6:19–21; see also Neh 10:29–30). Some English versions indicate that the celebrants included converts via a translation that runs something like: "The Israelites who had returned from exile, *together with* those who had joined them by separating themselves from the pollutions of the nations of the land to worship YHWH, the God of Israel, ate the Passover meal" (Ezra 6:21, emphasis added). Yet an equally possible translation of the original text is far less inclusive: "The Israelites who had returned from exile, *that is*, those who had joined them by separating themselves" (again, emphasis added). Given the exclusivist stance on communal membership in this section, confined as it is to documented genealogical ties, the second and less inclusive translation should be preferred.[50]

The rest of the books of Ezra and Nehemiah both nuance and radicalize these requirements for communal inclusion. As texts written from a first-person perspective and thus sometimes called the "Ezra Memoir" (Ezra 7–10 and Nehemiah 8–9) and the "Nehemiah Memoir (Nehemiah 1–7; 10–13), they offer a sympathetic portrayal of leaders who come back to the community from exile. The text is clear that both Ezra and Nehemiah came to Yehud long after the "first wave" of returnees who responded to Cyrus's edict around 539 BCE. In addition, Nehemiah also leaves Yehud after his first mission is complete and returns to the Persian court, only to return again after a time (Neh 13:6–7). With this experience of heroes arising from foreign lands and coming to Yehud generations after the time of forced migration, the text promotes the experience of return as a key factor in communal membership but doesn't specify it as a requirement. Indeed, there is a sense that the diaspora is a source for the true orthodoxy. As with the list of the community in Ezra 2 and Nehemiah 7, the books give several examples of the incorporation of people into the community in Yehud who arrived after the time of Cyrus.

The issue of group identity continues as a key theme throughout the memoirs, and emerges in a particularly disturbing way at the end of both narratives when the community attempts to forcibly evict "foreign" wives and children from their midst (Ezra 9–10 and Neh 13:23–29).[51] The men who married women outside of the group are accused of "faithlessness" (Ezra 9:2, 4; 10:2, 6; Neh 13:27), a key term that in postexilic literature refers to the offenses that brought about the exile. Although the offense is the same, the specific risk that such marriages pose is represented differently in both texts. In

---

50. Matthew Thiessen, "The Function of a Conjunction: Inclusivist or Exclusivist Strategies in Ezra 6.19-21 and Nehemiah 10.29-30?" *JSOT* 34, no. 1 (2009): 63–79.

51. It is likely that these "foreign women" were Yahwists who remained in the land during the exile.

Nehemiah, it is the loss of the Hebrew language that is threatened. Upon his discovery of intermarriage, Nehemiah exclaims that "half of their children spoke the language of Ashdod or the language of various peoples—they couldn't speak the language of Judah!" (Neh 13:23–24).[52] In Ezra, the impurity of the foreign women threatens contamination of the community. As the leaders present the issue, "the holy seed has mixed itself with the peoples of the lands" (Ezra 9:2). Ezra's prayer in response recounts an older warning to justify the ban on intermarriage: "The land that you are about to enter to possess is a land polluted with the pollutions of the peoples of the land . . . therefore, do not give your daughters to their sons" (Ezra 9:11–12). In the Hebrew Bible, this term for pollution usually refers only to women who are menstruating (Lev 12:5; 15:19; 18:19) who can themselves pollute men (Lev 15:24; 20:18).[53] The narratives give no indication that the foreign women were given the opportunity to incorporate into the community via rites of conversion found in texts such as Deuteronomy and Leviticus.[54] Rather, in both texts the threat to the community's identity via pollution or the loss of language means that the women must be purged so that the community can survive.[55]

It is true that these texts stand in clear contrast to other texts from this period, such as Chronicles and Ruth, that clearly promote the gifts that intermarriage with foreigners can entail. And the narratives in Ezra and Nehemiah themselves betray some amount of contradiction and tension in their accounts: since the intermarriage crisis erupts twice, it is clear that the entire community didn't fully embrace the text's presentation of the significance of the problem. And the texts don't actually narrate the sending away of the women, a situation that allows the reader a shred of possibility that the threatened expulsion didn't fully take place.[56] Nevertheless, the horror of these accounts cannot be denied, nor their use to legitimate racial

52. For more on this issue, see Katherine E. Southwood, "'And They Could Not Understand Jewish Speech': Language, Ethnicity, and Nehemiah's Intermarriage Crisis," *JTS* 62 (2011): 1–19.

53. Claudia Camp, *Wise, Strange, and Holy: The Strange Woman and the Making of the Bible*, JSOTSup 320, Gender, Culture Theory 9 (Sheffield: Sheffield Academic, 200), 33–34, n. 14.

54. Saul M. Olyan, *Rites and Rank: Hierarchy in Biblical Representations of Cult* (Princeton: Princeton University Press, 2000), 81–90; Saul M. Olyan, "Purity Ideology in Ezra-Nehemiah as a Tool to Reconstitute the Community," *JSJ* 35 (2004): 1–16.

55. David Janzen, "Scholars, Witches, Ideologues and What the Text Said: Ezra 9-10 and Its Interpretation," in *Approaching Yehud: New Approaches to the Study of the Persian Period*, ed. Jon L. Berquist (Atlanta: Society of Biblical Literature, 2007), 49–69.

56. Ezra 10:44 is often reconstructed to reflect a version of the text in 1 Esdras 9:36, "They

violence in later communities such as the treatment of the indigenous populations in Tongo or racial segregation in the United States.[57]

WOMEN IN 1–2 MACCABEES

Written to tell the story of Jewish revolt during a time of suppression under Greek-speaking rulers, 1–2 Maccabees (like 1–2 Chronicles) is mostly a story of men as rulers and warriors. Women are rarely mentioned, and appear in these narratives only "at the edges of the text."[58] Primarily they are wordless victims of war and harsh political policies. Along with children and cattle they are taken as booty by opposing armies as spoils of war (1 Macc 1:31–32; 8:10). They are also included in a stylized lament in the context of defeat: "Rulers and elders groaned. Young women and men became faint. The women's beauty faded. Every bridegroom was saddened, and intended brides sat mourning in their chambers" (1 Macc 1:26–27). Other laments portray the defeated city of Jerusalem as an abandoned mother and barren woman: "like a stranger to her offspring, and her children abandoned her. Her sanctuary was as barren as a desert. . . . Her dishonor became as great as her glory had been. Her joy turned into sadness" (1 Macc 1:38–40). Tellingly, the mother of the victorious Simon Maccabeus is first mentioned only *after* her death when we hear that her son built a pyramid for her tomb alongside her husband and sons (1 Macc 13:28).

There are two major exceptions to this portrayal of women as passive and silent victims. One is the report that women had circumcised their infant sons in disobedience to Antiochus's prohibition (1 Macc 1:60–61; cf. 2 Macc 6:10). Although neither their names nor their words are recorded, here the text gives a fleeting glimpse of female agency and resistance. The second is the much longer account of the Jewish mother who is martyred along with her

sent them away with their children." However, it is preferable to retain the ambiguity in the original text: "some of the women had set children."

57. Nasili Vakauta, "Myth of (Im)purity and the Peoples of the (Is)lands: A Fonua Reading of Ezra 9–10," *Pacific Journal of Theology* 42 (2009): 40–62; Cheryl B. Anderson, "Reflections in an Interethnic/racial Era on Interethnic/racial Marriage in Ezra," in *They Were All Together in One Place? Toward Minority Biblical Criticism*, ed. Randall C. Bailey et al. (Atlanta: Society of Biblical Literature, 2009), 47–64.

58. The phrase is from Claudia Rakel, "1 Maccabees: Women's Existence at the Edges of the Text," in *Feminist Biblical Interpretation: A Compendium of Critical Commentary on the Books of the Bible and Related Literature*, ed. Luise Schottroff and Marie-Theres Wacker, trans. Lisa E. Dahill et al. (Grand Rapids: Eerdmans, 2012), 483–91.

sons when they refuse to eat pork (2 Maccabees 7). One by one she witnesses their slow and gruesome deaths, but encourages them with "her womanly reasoning and manly courage" (2 Macc 7:21). When Antiochus asks her to counsel her seventh and only surviving son to relent, she agrees, only to backtrack on her word and use the occasion to spur him on to faithfulness: "Son, pity me who carried you in the womb nine months. . . . Accept death so that by God's mercy I may recover you with your brothers" (2 Macc 7:27–29).

In a context of brutal oppression, such accounts of courage are stirring. And the extended speech of the mother in 2 Maccabees 7 might inspire our imagination as we consider the brave but silent women, children, and men in the rest of the narratives who die for their faith. Written decades after the actual events, the narratives reflect a stereotypical portrait of women's experience—either as mute victims of male violence or as mothers leveraging their "womanly reasoning" and experience of pregnancy to motivate resistance. Yet these stories of triumph and despair also witness to God's ongoing presence with all those who suffer at the hands of empire, and remind us that sometimes the defiance of oppression (whether in silence or in speech) is remembered by future generations.

Like the other historical narratives, 1–2 Maccabees reminds us that the retelling of history serves a purpose in the present. Accounts of the past are not neutral or changeless but rather flexible venues for enshrining current values. Although they may provide clues for the period that they describe, they reveal at least as much about the author's goals and projects as they do about the later groups that adopted and canonized the texts. As such, it should not come as a surprise that diverse points of view are detectable in the texts since different communities manifest different concerns and values. Both 1–2 Chronicles and Ezra and Nehemiah promote a biological connection to the families of the past, as seen in their presentation of lists of names. But the family tree in 1 Chronicles 1–9 promotes the value of foreigners marrying into the family and highlights the relation of the nation to the world, whereas the lists of the returnees in Ezra 2 and Nehemiah 7 narrow the community to those who can document their relation to those who returned to Yehud from the exile. Similarly, Chronicles, Ezra, and Nehemiah all highlight the role of Yehud and Jerusalem as a core marker of the nation. But whereas the Chronicler promotes worship in the city as a mechanism to incorporate outsiders into the community, Ezra and Nehemiah add the experience of exile in Babylon as well as return to the land as constitutive for communal membership. Contemporary readers will want to question the narrow focus on male rulers and consider the texts from the untold perspective of the entire ancient community. They will also want to explore the historical narratives to see what they reveal about the time they present and the time in which they were written.

FOR FURTHER READING

Austern, Linda Phyllis, Kari Boyd McBride, and David L. Orvis, eds. *Psalms in the Early Modern World.* Burlington, VT: Ashgate, 2011.

Bail, Ulrike. "The Psalms: 'Who Is Speaking May Be *All* That Matters." In *Feminist Biblical Interpretation: A Compendium of Critical Commentary on the Books of the Bible and Related Literature,* edited by Luise Schottroff and Marie-Theres Wacker, 240–54. Translated by Lisa A. Dahill et al. Grand Rapids: Eerdmans, 2012.

Bloch, Chana, and Ariel Bloch. *The Song of Songs: The World's First Great Love Poem.* New York: Random House, 2006.

Camp, Claudia V. "Woman Wisdom." In *Women in Scripture,* edited by Carol Meyers, 548–52. Boston: Houghton Mifflin, 2000.

Chittister, Joan. *The Story of Ruth: Twelve Moments in Every Woman's Life.* Grand Rapids: Eerdmans, 2000.

Crawford, Sidnie White. "Esther." In *Women in Scripture,* edited by Carol Meyers, 74–78. Boston: Houghton Mifflin, 2000.

———. "Esther." In *Women's Bible Commentary,* edited by Carol A. Newsom, Sharon H. Ringe, and Jacqueline E. Lapsley, 201–7. Louisville: Westminster John Knox, 2012.

Davis, Ellen, and Margaret Adams Parker. *Who Are You, My Daughter? Reading Ruth Through Image and Text.* Louisville: Westminster John Knox, 2003.

Exum, J. Cheryl. *Song of Songs.* Louisville: Westminster John Knox, 2005.

———. "Song of Songs." In *Women's Bible Commentary,* edited by Carol A. Newsom, Sharon H. Ringe, and Jacqueline E. Lapsley, 247–54. Louisville: Westminster John Knox, 2012.

Fentress-Williams, Judy. *Ruth.* Nashville: Abingdon, 2012.

———. "Esther." In the *Old Testament and Apocrypha: Fortress*

Commentary on the Bible, edited by Gale A. Yee, Hugh R. Page Jr., and Matthew J. M. Coomber, 487–93. Minneapolis: Fortress Press, 2014.

Gerber, Christiane. "2 Maccabees: The Teaching of History." In *Feminist Biblical Interpretation: A Compendium of Critical Commentary on the Books of the Bible and Related Literature*, edited by Luise Schottroff and Marie-Theres Wacker, 492–503. Translated by Lisa E. Dahill et al. Grand Rapids: Eerdmans, 2012.

Hawkins, Peter, and Lesleigh Cushing Stahlberg. *Scrolls of Love: Ruth and the Song of Songs.* New York: Fordham University Press, 2006.

Knoppers, G. N. "Intermarriage, Social Complexity, and Ethnic Diversity in the Genealogy of Judah." *JBL* 120 (2001): 15–30.

Knowles, Melody D. "Ethics in Ezra and Nehemiah." In *Oxford Encyclopedia of the Bible and Ethics*, edited by Robert Brawley et al., 264–68. New York: Oxford University Press, 2014.

———. "Feminist Interpretation of the Psalms." In *The Oxford Handbook of the Psalms*, edited by William P. Brown, 424–36. Oxford: Oxford University Press, 2014.

Labahn, Antje, and Ehud Ben Zvi. "Observations on Women in the Genealogies of 1 Chronicles 1-9." *Biblica* 84, no. 4 (2003): 457–78.

Newsom, Carol. *The Book of Job: A Contest of Moral Imaginations.* New York: Oxford University Press, 2003.

———. "Job" in *Women's Bible Commentary*. Edited by Carol A. Newsom, Sharon H. Ringe, and Jacqueline E. Lapsley. Louisville: Westminster John Knox, 2012

Oegema, Gerbern S. "Portrayals of Women in 1 and 2 Maccabees." In *Transformative Encounters: Jesus and Women Re-viewed*, edited by Ingrid Rosa Kitzberger, 245–64. Leiden: Brill, 2000.

Rakel, Claudia. "1 Maccabees: Women's Existence at the Edges of the Text." In *Feminist Biblical Interpretation: A Compendium of Critical Commentary on the Books of the Bible and Related Literature*, edited by Luise Schottroff and Marie-Theres Wacker, 483–91. Translated by Lisa E. Dahill et al. Grand Rapids: Eerdmans, 2012.

Sakenfeld, Katharine D. *Just Wives? Stories of Power and Survival in the Old Testament and Today.* Louisville: Westminster John Knox, 2003.

———. *Ruth.* Interpretation: A Bible Commentary for Teaching and Preaching. Louisville: Westminster John Knox, 1989.

Schroer, Silvia. "'Under the Shadow of Your Wings': The Metaphor of God's Wings in the Psalms, Exodus 19.4, Deuteronomy 32.11 and Malachi 3.20, as Seen Through the Perspectives of Feminism and the History of Religion." In *Wisdom and Psalms*, edited by Athalya Brenner and Carole R. Fontaine, 264–82. Feminist Companion to the Bible 2. Sheffield: Sheffield Academic, 1998.

Southwood, Katherine. *Ethnicity and the Mixed Marriage Crisis in Ezra 9-10: An Anthropological Approach.* Oxford: Oxford University Press, 2012.

Tanner, Beth LaNeel. *The Book of Psalms through the Lens of Intertextuality.* Studies in Biblical Literature 26. New York: Peter Lang, 2001.

Trible, Phyllis. "Two Women in a Man's World: A Reading of the Book of Ruth." *Soundings: An Interdisciplinary Journal* 59, no. 3 (Fall 1976): 251–79.

Wacker, Marie-Theres. "Books of Chronicles: In the Vestibule of Women." In *Feminist Biblical Interpretation: A Compendium of Critical Commentary on the Books of the Bible and Related Literature,* edited by Luise Schottroff and Marie-Theres Wacker, 178–91. Translated by Lisa E. Dahill et al. Grand Rapids: Eerdmans, 2012.

Yoder, Christine Roy. "Proverbs." In *Women's Bible Commentary,* edited by Carol A. Newsom, Sharon H. Ringe, and Jacqueline E. Lapsley, 232–42. Louisville: Westminster John Knox, 2012.

Contributors

Corrine L. Carvalho, professor of biblical studies, University of St. Thomas

Judy Fentress-Williams, professor of Old Testament, Virginia Theological Seminary

Melody D. Knowles, vice president for Academic Affairs and associate professor of Old Testament, Virginia Theological Seminary

Vanessa Lovelace, associate professor of Hebrew Bible, Interdenominational Theological Center, Atlanta, Georgia

Carolyn J. Sharp, professor of homiletics, Yale Divinity School

Gale A. Yee, Nancy W. King Professor of Biblical Studies *Emerita*, Episcopal Divinity School

Index of Names & Subjects

Deborah, 23, 86, 88–89. *See also*
    Female prophets
Deconstructive criticism, 22–24
Delilah, 23, 26n86, 92
Deuteronomist (Dtr), 75, 79,
    86–87, 90–91, 93, 96, 100,
    102–3
Deuteronomistic History (DH),
    vii, 75–76, 78, 100–101, 103
Deuteronomy, 45, 62, 68–69, 75,
    78, 80–82, 164
Diaspora, 138, 141, 143, 158, 163
Dill, Bonnie Thornton, 2n4
Dinah, 52–53
Discourse, 6, 23, 55, 58, 62, 78, 90
Dishonor, 94, 165. See Honor/
    dishonor
Dissent, 42, 44–45, 57–58, 62, 68
Divine Warrior, 58, 82, 113
Divorce, 69
Donaldson, Laura E., 35–36
Dube, Musa W., 28, 34–35, 85
Duffey, Eamon, 156n35
Dworkin, Andrea, 4

Edwards, Katie B., 27n90
Eisenbaum, Pamela, 144n7
Elijah, 101
Elimelech, 138
Elisha, 100
Elites: male, 108, 117; men, 117;
    ruling, 99; female, 36
Embodiment, 147
Endor, woman at, 96. *See also*
    Woman necromancer
Epistemology, 5
Esau, 51
Esther, viii, 24, 29, 138, 141–43,
    155

Ethnicity, vii, 2, 29, 32–34, 78,
    87–88, 125–26
Eunuchs, 121, 123. *See also*
    Castration
Eve, 14–16, 19; Adam and Eve,
    27, 48
Exile, forced migration, 119, 126,
    159, 163
Exiles, return of the, 120, 126,
    161–62
Exodus, book of, 18, 35, 45, 54,
    57–62, 66, 84, 87, 114, 127
Exogamy, 78, 80, 100
Exum, J. Cheryl, 26
Ezekiel, 36, 108, 110, 112–18,
    122–23, 126, 129
Ezekiel's wife, 120, 126
Ezra, 31, 158, 160–66
Ezra Memoir, 163

Father, 4n8, 19, 36, 51, 82, 91–92,
    100, 115, 117, 146, 148
Female priests/priestess, 117, 123
Female prophets, 115–16. *See also*
    Deborah, Huldah
Femininity, 121
Feminism, definition of, 1. *See also*
    liberal feminism, Marxist
    feminism, postmodern
    feminism, queer theory,
    radical feminism
Feminist biblical scholarship, ix,
    1–2, 10, 12–14, 25, 47, 54, 66,
    124; historical–critical
    approaches, 17, 37, 42;
    interdisciplinary approaches,
    vii, 22, 37; intersectional
    approaches, 37, 126, 128;
    literary-critical approaches,